# Christian Chick's Guide to Surviving Divorce

## What Your Girlfriends Would Tell You If They Knew What To Say

## Suzanne Reeves

Lighthouse Publishing
of the Carolinas

www.lighthousepublishingofthecarolinas.com

# Praise for *Christian Chick's Guide to Surviving Divorce*

"Divorce impacts everyone, even Christians. *The Christian Chick's Guide to Surviving Divorce* is a crucial resource for any woman of faith during such a difficult time. It will inspire and encourage you and probably make you laugh a little – all on a journey towards healing and wholeness."

**W. Terry Whalin,**
acquisitions editor and author of Jumpstart Your Publishing Dreams, www.jumpstartyourpublishingdreams.com

"Raw honesty, conversational style, and ability to find humor in her experiences make this book read like a letter from a dear friend who understands. Suzanne Reeves has repurposed her own pain into coaching other women through the emotional struggle, shame, and discouragement of divorce to find the courage to move forward."

**Michelle Rayburn,**
speaker, author of *The Repurposed and Upcycled Life.*
www.michellerayburn.com

"I started reading and couldn't put the book down. It is an easy read and filled with such love and encouragement. Suzanne has walked through the fire of divorce but doesn't smell like smoke. She has emerged on top as one Perky Texan."

**MaryElaine Cline,**
minister and international director

"A must read for any woman going through a divorce. Encouraging and practical with humor to leaven the lumps divorce leaves. Suzanne tackles the tough issues with wisdom and grace to help women navigate one of the toughest times of their lives. We all know someone who needs this book – if it's you, you've found help from just the right girlfriend!"

**Maggie Wallem Rowe,**
author and speaker

THE CHRISTIAN CHICK'S GUIDE TO SURVIVING DIVORCE –
WHAT YOUR GIRLFRIENDS WOULD TELL YOU IF THEY KNEW
WHAT TO SAY BY SUZANNE REEVES

Published by Lighthouse Publishing of the Carolinas
2333 Barton Oaks Dr., Raleigh, NC, 27614
ISBN 978-1-938499-74-6
Copyright © 2013 by Suzanne Reeves
Cover design by Ted Ruybal, www.wisdomhousebooks.com
Interior design by Reality Info Systems, www.realityinfo.com
Available in print from your local bookstore, online, or from the publisher
at: www.lighthousepublishingofthecarolinas.com

For more information on this book and the author visit:
www.suzannereeves.com

Brought to you by the creative team at LighthousePublishingoftheCarolinas.
com:
Eddie Jones, Amberlyn Edwards, Brian Cross, Rowena Kuo, and Meaghan
Burnett

Library of Congress Cataloging-in-Publication Data
Reeves, Suzanne.
The Christian Chick's Guide to Surviving Divorce – What Your Girlfriends
Would Tell You if They Knew What to Say / Suzanne Reeves, 1st ed.

Printed in the United States of America

# TABLE OF CONTENTS

**Introduction**

**Addressing the Pain**

**Learn!**

**Moving on Towards Triumph**

**Thanks**

# DEDICATION

To my precious sisters in this journey -
May you know God's love in the depths of pain,
May you hear that it will not always be this hard,
May you see that you will be okay,
And may joy once again be part of your story.

# DISCLAIMER

The very nature of a divorce means conflict. In writing this book, it was not my desire or goal to stir up more conflict—I've had enough to last two lifetimes. Actually, it was the opposite. I want to help other women who are going through their own difficult situations by sharing how I survived mine. The memories and experiences of my divorce and the years leading up to it are my own. It is not my desire to bash my ex-husband or paint him in a bad light. Divorces are complicated, and everyone grows and changes through the tragedies in life. I am not the same person I was pre-divorce, and neither is my ex-husband. In an effort to respect the privacy of so many wounded people, all the names as well as identifying characteristics have been changed.

*Chapter 1*

# HE'S NOT REALLY GOING TO LEAVE, IS HE?

"You two have a lot in common," my friend introduces me to her girlfriend. Then our mutual friend nods and gives me *the look*. Ahh. I understand *the look*. That's code for: Please Help Her, She's Going Through a Terrible Divorce and I Don't Know What to Say to Her But I Hope You Can Figure Something Out Since You Seemed to Turn Out Somewhat Okay. This casual introduction, followed by the coded *look*, happens to me about once a week.

In my circles, everyone appeared happily married. Five years into my marriage, I would have described myself that way as well. I didn't know anyone my age who was divorced. All my friends were celebrating their tenth wedding anniversaries and expecting their second or third child. But not me.

While I attended their baby showers and celebrated

1

their anniversaries, my own marriage was crumbling. My marriage was spiraling downward, and I couldn't seem to stop it.

What's your story? Is your divorce a public one? Or is it a private pain that no one knows about? Have you made some horrible mistakes, or have you been blindsided by a spouse hell-bent on leaving? Are you officially divorced, or are you living in a thin excuse for a marriage? Our stories may not be the same. We may not come from the same situations or backgrounds. But, if we share the pain of divorce or the impending specter of it, then my precious friend, we do indeed have much in common.

And for that, I am so sorry. I am so sorry that you are going through this tragedy of divorce. I am so sorry for the pain you have experienced. I am so sorry that divorce has become part of your life's journey. But know this: you may be going through the valley, but you are not alone. Thousands have walked before you, and thousands will walk after you. I am praying for you as I write this very sentence.

And most importantly, God is with you! Despite what you may be feeling right now, you are not alone. Our God is bigger than whatever it is you are going through. And you will go *through*. Not go into and wallow around in suffering there forever, but through. Through to come out on the other side. You can make it! You are going to be okay. I know, because I went through it. And I'm okay.

* * *

"He's not going to leave you."

My mom tried to reassure me with these words. At the time, I found them comforting. She had to be right, of course. My husband whom I loved with all my heart would never leave. I was eight months pregnant with our first child. He wouldn't leave me, right? I mean, things had been rough the past few months, but not so bad that he would... I couldn't even bring myself to consider the thought. We had a baby coming. We had graduated from Wheaton College, that bastion of Christendom. My husband played in the worship band at church on Sunday mornings.

"He's not going to leave you," she said again.

But slowly, things got worse and worse. As I watched our marriage become a phantom of its very self, I realized that my husband might indeed leave me. The same man I loved so much that I willingly left my tight-knit family and moved a thousand miles away to be with him. The good-looking senior who visited me in the hospital my freshman year of college. The husband who tenderly painted my toenails and was a fabulous cook. The man who sent my spirits soaring the first time he kissed me. The husband who joined me in picking out our new puppy together. The newlywed with whom I had successfully wallpapered, for Pete's sake! The handsome man in a black tuxedo to whom I had promised to be faithful. This very same man, my husband, the love of my life, might leave me.

I might be divorced.

The day I finally acknowledged that things might end in the worst possible way was pretty rough. I felt like if I didn't give breath to the thought, then it wouldn't happen. But I couldn't deny the reality any more. It was a very difficult day when I realized that maybe God wasn't going to rescue my marriage after all. That all those hours I spent on my knees begging for my marriage—often joined by godly prayer warriors— might be answered with a no.

Divorce was spoken of in hushed tones when I was growing up. In elementary school, we had only one girl in our class whose parents were divorced. And even back then, I remember an undercurrent of disdain for her and her single mom. How pompous, how judgmental I had been. Was I now going to experience the disdain that I had so easily given out, even as a child? Father, forgive me. Oh the painful, shameful irony.

In high school, my world broadened a bit. Some of our close family friends went through divorces. And sadly, it was becoming more common in all layers of society. I now had friends who were enduring the agony of parents splitting up.

I am one of the lucky ones. My parents have an amazing marriage. I didn't appreciate until college how blessed I was to grow up in a home where God was first and everything else followed. My parents are certainly not perfect, but they are godly, and they deeply love each other. Their marriage is a shining example of what one should look like. I felt well prepared.

So when I said, "I do" in front of all our friends and family, it really was forever—no matter what.

I believed my husband when he said the same words.

\* \* \*

*This is really going to happen,* I remember thinking one day. *This madness is not a dream. Phil is really going to divorce me. I am going to be divorced. I am going to be a divorcee.*

Divorcee.

What an awful word. Images of the desperate neighbor down the street who answers the door in a negligee come to mind. Oh no. Not me. You've got the wrong girl, God. This is me, remember? Suzanne. You know, the girl from a great Christian home: The girl who could say all the books of the Bible by second grade. I went to private Christian schools. I went to Wheaton College! People from Wheaton don't get divorced. People with my pedigree don't get divorced. Check your files, Lord. You've got the wrong gal.

But He didn't have the wrong gal. For, after four years of dating, five happy years of marriage, and almost four more long years of misery, the judge took his glasses off, pronounced our marriage dissolved, and I was divorced.

* * *

I hate how you are often forced to define yourself by your marriage status. I never really cared or noticed before. Now, I have to check the "Divorced" box on whatever form I'm filling out. But all they give you is a box. No place to clarify. No place to explain how hard you fought. No place to say how painful it is. Only a label: Divorced.

I had to make the decision that I will not let a label define me. I will not be defined by my marital status. My divorce will always be a part of my make-up, and it will always be a part of my history, but it is not me! I will always bear the scars, but they are not who I am. My precious friend, don't let the scars define you. They will always be there. But they are not who you are.

Early on, I decided to choose life. By God's grace, I choose life. Daily, sometimes hourly, I choose life. Through the pain and the tears, I choose life. Because of who my God is, I choose life.

*I have set before you life and death, blessings and curses. Now choose life, so that you and your children may live...* Deuteronomy 30:19b

I want to live, my friend. Join me in the land of the living. Take the first step toward healing. Right now, in this very moment, choose life. No matter what your circumstances, you can choose life. If you are sliding down the slippery path toward divorce, choose life. If you receive a knock at the door and a sheriff is standing there with those horrible papers, choose life. If you see your mate walking around town with another woman, choose life. If you have to sell your house, your car and your wedding ring, choose life. God is hope—He is life! If you can do nothing else, if you can't get out of bed, if you can't even pray—take the first small step with me today. Right now. Choose life.

ADDRESSING THE PAIN

_Chapter 2_

# OUCH, MY HEART HURTS

There is no way around it. Divorce is an excruciating process. It just is. Occasionally, you hear of the "amicable divorce." A divorce where both parties mutually end things, claim they're better for it, and stay friends after the papers are signed. But I think that's a load of hooey. Even when both parties are in agreement and things go smoothly, it still hurts. And that's the "good" kind of divorce.

Then, there's the other kind of divorce: the divorce where every day is painful. The hurt so agonizing, sometimes you feel actual physical pain. Is that what's happening to you? Do you feel like your heart is literally breaking in half? Oh my friend, I have been there.

There were months at a time that I couldn't make it through a single hymn or chorus at church without weeping. I remember sitting in my Sunday school class with an empty chair next to me, tears streaming down

8

my face. It was so good to be in church, but man, it hurt to be there alone.

The commercials at Christmas taunted me with their happy couples blissfully in love. Wonderful men buying fabulous diamonds for their beautiful wives, while the snow softly fell under the street lamp. I wanted to throw up.

I remember the pain of seeing my husband show kindness to a dear friend of ours, wishing he would be kind to me.

And then, there was the day in the midst of the whole awful process when I couldn't take it anymore.

Phil had just stormed out of the house, furious at me because I caught him in a lie about his female dinner companion the previous evening. Our one-month-old baby girl slept in the next room. The door slammed behind him, and I heard him peel out of the driveway. I was in shock, completely overwhelmed by the anger and lies.

When I found out he lied to me, it took all of my courage to confront him. I agonized over the right thing to do. Do I risk his wrath, or should I just let it slide? Will he admit his lie, and then maybe we can start working our way back from these depths of marriage despair? Or will this be the final straw that pushes him to leave me? I wanted so badly to reach out to him, to work things out. I wanted so badly to save our marriage.

I felt numb as I listened at the door of Molly's nursery, hoping she wasn't awakened by his tirade. I turned away from her door, stumbled into our bedroom, and collapsed on the floor next to our bed. I was beyond myself. All the pain of the previous year exploded, and I couldn't get off the floor. I remember the smell of the carpet as I sobbed and sobbed, my face buried in the fibers. I wept out loud in agony and confusion. I wept for my husband who had become a stranger. I wept for my infant daughter in the next room. And I wept under the crushing pain of rejection and abandonment from the man who had promised to cherish me.

I know what it is like to hurt, my precious friend. I know what immobilizing pain feels like. I have been there. If you are there today, I am so sorry. I am so sorry that you are hurting. Oh my friend, I would lay on the floor and cry with you. Perhaps you have a good friend you can call. Or perhaps you have no one. Whatever your circumstances, I want you to know, you are not alone.

I was not alone as I lay moaning on the floor. My Father was there with me. He held me close while I cried it out, He rocked me as I was racked with sobs of grief, and He comforted me as my weeping consumed my very breath. He didn't take away the pain, but He did carry me through it. God was with me that day, the day my grief and agony spilled over. And He is with you too. God sees every single tear you cry. He bottles them up, and He holds them close to His heart.* He feels the torment with you. He weeps for you. And He longs for you to run to Him.

These are not empty placations. These are deep truths. I know, because I have been there.

"But you don't know my situation," you say. "You don't know what I have been through." And you are right. That is true. I do not know your exact situation. I am not walking in your shoes.

But, I have walked a similar journey in my own lonely shoes of grief. That day, as my tears soaked the carpet, the only one I could turn to was God. I cried out to my Heavenly Father. And I cried out to His beautiful son, Jesus. The only one who could truly walk with me was my sweet Jesus, for He knows all about pain as well.

Jesus knows what betrayal feels like. Judas, one of His twelve disciples—the closest friends Jesus had on earth—sold Him out for a bag of silver. Jesus knows first-hand what it's like to be rejected by those closest to Him. Another disciple, Peter, denied that he even knew Jesus. Jesus knows what it feels like to give everything you have, only to have it thrown back in your face, crucified by the same people who worshiped Him only days before. And He knows what it is like to face insurmountable odds. Jesus knows.

And my sweet friend, that is enough. You may not be

there yet. You may still feel so completely alone. But you are not. You are not alone in your sorrow. Eventually, you will understand that Jesus knows. And you will realize that is enough. As you weep on the carpet, or in your car, or in the restroom at your office, it is enough that Jesus is weeping with you. He is enough.

There was no way I could convey to someone what I went through day after day. I didn't call my friends for each painful barb that was thrown at me, for each crushing remark or devastating revelation. I couldn't. I couldn't make anyone understand how much it hurt. I couldn't rehash it all, and they wouldn't want to sit through it even if I could. You can't possibly make someone understand each painful event or emotion. Maybe you've tried. They just don't fully get it, do they? They can't. It's not because they don't care. It's because they just are not you. They are not equipped to feel your grief the same way you do. But Jesus can. It is enough that Christ knows your pain. He alone knows each tear you cry, each time your spirit is crushed, and each time the pain rocks you to the core. He knows. He understands. He has been there. And He is enough.

## The Time Has Come To Hand It Over

Are you ready to let Him be enough? Are you ready to hand over this whole awful mess? He wants it, you know. He wants you to give the pain over to Him and surrender the agony. His shoulders have carried agony before. This road of pain is not new to Him. He has walked it before, and He wants to walk it again with you. Give it all to Him. Your burden is too great for you to carry alone. It is just too much. Give it to Jesus. He wants to carry it for you.

*Come to me, all you who are weary and burdened. And I will give you rest.* Matthew 11:28

My precious friend, give all that pain to Jesus. Do it right now. Say it out loud. "Jesus, I'm giving you all my pain, all my burdens. Please take them and carry them for me."

Picture yourself physically handing over your burdens and laying them at the foot of the cross. Watch yourself as you set them down and then walk away. Take a deep breath. Breathe deeply for perhaps the first time in months, and release that pain. Do it again tomorrow. And the next day. Each day in its own time. Pour out your heart to Him. Let the pain go, and give it to Jesus. He is enough.

\* Based on Psalms 56:8

## Chapter 3

# LOVE NEVER FAILS

Here's the simple truth: God loves you.
Whether you're in a spot to hear it right now or
not, the truth remains: God loves you. That was hard for
me to hear, or more accurately, hard for me to process.
I went to church and sang songs about how much God
loved me. I could quote Bible verses proclaiming God's
love. But when it came down to it, did I really believe
that God loved me?

When you go through a divorce, your definition of
love gets skewed. Didn't we promise to love each other
no matter what? Didn't we say, "Until death do us part"
in front of God and everybody? Love was supposed to be
forever. I had no illusions that our married love would
be perfect, but I did expect it to last. I was planning on
being one of those cute old couples interviewed on their
820th wedding anniversary who chuckle and finish
each other's sentences, and when asked how they've

14

kept their love alive, he gently reaches for her hand and says something wise and profound about how they're still so in love with each other—and that he always lets her win the arguments.

But that's not how it went. Not at all. "I just don't love you anymore," Phil admitted when I confronted him on why he wasn't wearing his wedding ring. At first he lied and said he couldn't find it. What? But when I found his ring hidden on a shelf and handed it to him, he spoke those devastating words.

"What do you mean?" I wanted to scream. "What do you mean you don't love me anymore? I still love you. How can you not love me? I know I'm not perfect, but neither are you. And I've chosen to still love you. That's not an option for you—not loving me anymore is not an option! Remember? You promised to love me until we died—not until you didn't feel like it anymore."

"I'm sorry, but I'm just unhappy. Why would I want to wear something that just reminds me how unhappy I am?" he finished.

Ouch.

When your husband tells you he doesn't love you anymore, it wreaks havoc on your self-esteem. Your self-worth plunges down the toilet. You question everything about yourself and wonder if you even matter anymore. Deep down, I knew my value did not depend on my husband's love for me. But, the reality was, when he said those words to me, I was crushed.

Have you heard those same words from the man you love? Or you just know they are true—that your husband doesn't love you anymore. Are you in so much pain that you want to punch somebody when you hear the word "love"?

I was. So I went to the only place I knew I would find comfort. I opened up my Bible. "Jesus loves me, this I know. For the Bible tells me so..." the children's song says. Really? Did I really know that? I needed to see it in writing and feel it in my soul. In the midst of my tears, I desperately needed to know that someone still loved me.

And do you know what I found? The song was true. God loves me. And God loves you. Even if you don't feel it right now, it's still true. God loves you. It's right there. Verse after verse in the Bible talks about how much God loves you, how much He cares for you, and how precious you are to Him.

Just a short list to encourage you right now:

- *And hope does not disappoint us, because God has poured out his love into our hearts by the Holy Spirit, whom he has given us.* Romans 5:5
- *But God demonstrates his own love for us in this: While we were still sinners, Christ died for us.* Romans 5:8
- *For I am convinced that neither death nor life, neither angels nor demons, neither the present nor the future, nor any powers, neither height nor*

*depth, nor anything else in all creation, will be able to separate us from the love of God that is in Christ Jesus our Lord.* Romans 8:38-39
- *(And I pray that you) may have power, together with all the saints, to grasp how wide and long and high and deep is the love of Christ, and to know this love that surpasses knowledge—that you may be filled to the measure of all the fullness of God.* Ephesians 3:18-19
- *How great is the love the Father has lavished on us, that we should be called children of God! And that is what we are!* 1 John 3:1a

There are so many verses about God's love for you in the Bible, they could have their own book. See the appendix for even more verses of encouragement!

Here are some in particular that bring great hope:
- *For God so loved the world that he gave his one and only Son, that whoever believes in him shall not perish but have eternal life.* John 3:16

God loved you and me so much that He was willing to sacrifice His own son, Jesus, in order that we could spend eternity with Him.
- *For you created my inmost being; you knit me together in my mother's womb. I praise you because I am fearfully and wonderfully made; your works are wonderful, I know that full well.* Psalms 139:13-14

You are not just a cosmic accident. Did you know that God knew everything about you before you were born? And not only did He know everything about you, He designed and planned you. You are so important to Him that you have always been part of His original plan. When He drew up the universe—you were chosen by God to be in it. You are fearfully and wonderfully made.

Lord, I don't feel so wonderful sometimes. I really would have liked to have been at least 5'8" with gorgeous long legs. I'm barely 5ft. on a good hair day. And I think I would have picked blue eyes. My brown eyes are nice, but they're nothing special. And why was learning French so stinkin' hard? I like English, what went wrong in French? If I was only smarter, French would have been easy. And I really wish I weren't allergic to hay ... God smiles and gently points me back to the verse in Psalms. I am fearfully and wonderfully made. God knit me together in my mother's womb. What a tender picture of our sweet Lord thoughtfully and carefully placing each part of me and each part of you exactly where it is supposed to be. The love of a Creator for His Creation. God loves me. And God loves you.

If only I had lost that baby weight, maybe my husband wouldn't have left. I should have finished college, or gotten a Ph.D., or learned Swahili. Maybe if I had memorized the stats of every baseball team and pretended to like *The Three Stooges,* he would have stayed. Or, if I got plastic surgery to perk up, pinch in, or smooth out, maybe then my husband would love me. Ridiculous of course—or is it? I don't know why you and your husband are getting a divorce. Maybe the years haven't been kind, and that bedroom chemistry fizzled out years ago. Maybe he left you for the younger model down the street. Maybe he wants to talk about the latest advancements in electrical engineering or a Wall Street shake down, and you can't keep up. Do you look in the mirror, or at your bank account, or your list of accomplishments, and hate what you see?

*The LORD does not look at the things man looks at. Man looks at the outward appearance, but the LORD looks at the heart.* 1 Samuel 16:7b

God doesn't love you because of how you look, what position you hold, or what your earning power is. He really doesn't. He doesn't care if you're short or tall, if you have dandruff, or if you're double-jointed. He doesn't care if you have freckles, your teeth are straight, or your second toe is longer than your first (mine is by the way—fascinating, I know). Other than wanting you to be healthy and take good care of the body He designed for you, God does not love you because of what you look like. Nor does He care what level of education you achieved and whether or not the title of Diaper Changer headlines your resume. God loves you because you are His child, and He fearfully and wonderfully made you.

So give yourself a break. Stop being critical of what you see in the mirror, don't hide when other people can actually carry on a conversation in French, and stop comparing yourself to every woman who swishes down the street. God is not doing that to you, so don't do it to yourself. God loved you enough to plan you from the beginning of time. He lovingly designed you. Because God loves you, you have value! Because God designed you, you are beautiful! And because God sent Jesus to die for you, you have self-worth!

Remember my basic brown eyes? They're not so basic—they're actually pretty amazing. The human eye processes 36,000 pieces of data per hour. It can distinguish between 500 shades of gray. One eyeball contains six million cone cells that help us see color, and 125 million rod cells that help us see at night. Your eye muscles are some of the most powerful muscles in the human body—100 times stronger than they need to be. And in optimum conditions, the human eye can see the light from one candle fourteen miles away. Wow!

If God put so much care, thought, and power into your eyeball, think about how much effort and creativity He put into the whole you. He loves every amazing thing about you, all the individual parts, and most importantly, God loves the whole package. You are precious in His sight!

*The LORD your God is with you, he is mighty to save.*
*He will take great delight in you, he will quiet you*

*with his love, he will rejoice over you with singing.*
Zephaniah 3:17

That little verse from Zephaniah is my favorite verse in the whole Bible. The Bible is filled with verses about worshiping God and singing praises to Him, but this verse shows the Creator rejoicing over His Creation. "He will rejoice over you with singing." When Molly was a baby, I found myself just singing to her. Singing over her for the pure joy of my child. I wasn't singing over her because she had done amazing things; in those early days, all she did was eat, poop, and cry. I wasn't singing over her because of how she looked; although I thought she was adorable, she didn't have any hair until she was almost three years old. I was singing over her because she was mine. My heart was overflowing with love so intense, so consuming, that it could only be expressed in song.

This is how your Heavenly Father loves you: with intense, passionate, all-consuming, utter joy! His father's heart overflows in song because of how much He loves you. Take that to your heart today, sweet friend.

\*\*\*

But what if you haven't always loved God in return? Maybe your spiritual journey got hijacked along the way, or never really started in the first place. What if the only thing you know about God's love has been

21

distorted by people in your life who promised to love you?

The Bible is full of parables, stories told by Jesus with a deeper meaning, demonstrating God's love. In one of my favorite ones about the prodigal son, Jesus paints a deeply touching picture of how passionately God loves us.

A rich young son demands his inheritance from his father while the father is still living. In the Hebrew culture, not only was this selfish, it was akin to saying that the father was dead to the son. But, the father gave him what he wished. The son left home and squandered the entire fortune given to him. Starving and living among pigs, (it doesn't get any worse for a Jew) the son decides to go back home and beg for work as a servant in his father's household.

The Bible says: *But while he was still a long way off, his father saw him and was filled with compassion for him; he ran to his son, threw his arms around him and kissed him.*\* Oh hurting friend, this is the same Father who is standing watch for you. Whether you have been away for a long time, or you are simply a child in pain, your Father is watching for you. He is waiting for you. And when He sees you begin to approach Him, He runs to you. He longs to throw His arms around you and hold you close.

When your husband tells you he doesn't love you anymore, God still loves you. When you feel like you are worthless, God is watching at the gate for you. When you can't take another step, God is running to you.

Fall into the arms of your Father, sweet friend. For there, you will find the love your heart so desperately longs for. God's love will never fail. He will always be faithful to you. He will never leave you.

God loves you.

* This parable is from Luke 15, which also has two other wonderful parables about God's love for us.

LEARN!

## Chapter 4

# PITCHING YOUR TENT AT CAMP WILDERNESS

Life is full of gentle teachable moments. And then, there are the moments that bash you on the head. Welcome to Camp Wilderness. Camp Wilderness is a place of instruction, and it's not the gentle, teachable moments kind of instruction. That was back down the road at Camp Cream Puff. Camp Wilderness is the place of intense learning of the refining-fire kind. It's a lonely, desolate place where there's no toilet paper and definitely no air conditioning. "Whoa!" you say, "I didn't sign up for this camp. I don't want to be here."

Neither did I. But I was. As my world crumbled around me, I found myself pitching a tent at Camp Wilderness. I was moving in whether I wanted to or not. They had my reservation, and I had no say, no voice in the matter. The only choice I had was what I would do with my time there.

By the grace of the Holy Spirit, I chose to learn. Precious sister in Christ, ask Him for this grace to learn. Choose to learn through the pain. Don't waste your time in camp. Early on, I determined to learn everything God was trying to teach me. I didn't want to miss a single lesson. If I had no choice but to trek through Camp Wilderness, I only wanted to go this route once.

Pain can be a powerful teacher. How many times does a child have to put his hand on a hot stove to realize that's a bad idea? How many times does a speeder have to get a ticket before they slow down? (For some of us, more than we'd like to admit.) How many times does God have to rattle your cage before you will listen to Him?

My friend, do you realize God is trying to get your attention? Choose right now to learn what the Father has for you. He will not give up teaching you, but don't go this route again. Don't waste this opportunity. Ask the Holy Spirit what He wants to teach you. And then, learn.

***

I suppose God had been trying to get my attention for a while, but I don't know because I wasn't listening closely. I was happy in my marriage to Phil, content with the status quo, and generally well on my way to a perfect life. We had just moved into a bigger house in a nicer suburb, Phil's job was improving as he was climbing up the corporate ladder, and we were pregnant with our first child. Things were going great—just like I had planned, really. It was nice of God to go along with my plan.

But looking back, I had gotten too comfortable. Dare I say, lukewarm? There was nothing particularly bad about me. I was a solid Christian by all respects. I loved the Lord, regularly went to church, and served frequently in many capacities. I was not ashamed of being a Christian. I talked often of my faith in God and even led a few people to Christ.

But God wanted more. He wanted more of my heart, more of me. He wanted me to deeply and passionately love Him with everything I had. He had tried to instruct and guide me with the gentle whisper route, but I didn't hear Him. I wasn't listening closely enough to Him to hear the gentle whisper. I was happily going along in my clueless life—but God was about to kick up the lesson plan.

So now you find yourself here in this desolate place just as I did. What is God trying to teach you? What does He want you to know? What is so important that He has allowed your world to be turned upside down? The following chapters dive deep into the lessons learned at Camp Wilderness.

Listen, my sweet friend. Be teachable. Camp Wilderness is a place of difficult lessons, but also a place of tremendous personal growth. Unzip that tent, fall on your knees, and listen for the voice of God.

*Chapter 5*

# GOD HASN'T LEFT—HE IS STILL ON THE THRONE

Lord, where are you? Are you seeing what's happening to me? And more to the point, why aren't you doing anything about it? Are you hearing my prayers, Lord? I am begging you to save my marriage! Why aren't things getting better? Are you even listening?

God, you can do anything. Anything! You don't have to change the course of history here. I'm not asking for world peace. Just please, please cause my husband to re-think what he is doing. Throw him a bump in the road—something to get his attention. Anything. Go into that cold hard place where his heart used to be and light a spark of love. Lord, make my husband love me again.

I wondered if God was even out there, if He was even hearing me. Perhaps you have had a conversation with God like that—wondering if He was listening, if

He even cared. Have you struggled in the silent nights? In the times where the tick tock of the clock echoing in an empty house was enough to make you scream?

Those were my moments. Maybe they are yours too.

But God, if you knew Phil was going to leave me, why did you let us get married in the first place? In church, in Your Name no less? You could have stopped our marriage. I could have gotten the measles the day before. He could have gotten cold feet—which, although painful at the time, would have been a much better option than getting divorced several years later.

In fact, why did you even let us meet in the first place? You knew I would fall madly in love with him. You knew I would leave my family and move a thousand miles away from my home for him. You knew we would make a baby together.

And you knew he would crush me.

Oh my friend, are you in the pit of despair? That place where every time you turn around, there's a new, and even deeper, pain. Are you crying out to God, and He's not answering?

Despair is a terrifying place to be. Despair is when you long for your husband to come home from work—hoping he'll walk through the door and just hold you—but you know he's "going out" instead. And when you ask him with whom or how long he'll be out, he accuses you of being nosy and controlling. Or worse, he just ignores you altogether.

Despair is when you go to pay for groceries, and your credit card is declined. "But I don't understand," you implore the clerk, "We have a $15,000 limit." And he shrugs and hands it back to you. You leave the store empty-handed, wondering what to make your kids for dinner.

Despair is when the bank calls and says your mortgage hasn't been paid for the last three months. Your husband has always paid the mortgage and handled all the bills. What other bills haven't been paid? Where does he even put them? And what happened to all the money?

Despair is watching your son's face fall when he scans the bleachers at his soccer game, only to realize his dad didn't show up—again.

Despair is when you find a small wrapped gift in your husband's coat pocket—with the name of another woman on it. And it's your birthday tomorrow.

Sweet friend, cling to the Lord in the midst of your despair. Although it may seem like it, God has not forgotten you. He has not abandoned you.

*I will never leave you nor forsake you.* Joshua 1:5b

God says this phrase five different places in the Bible. Five times!* He will never leave us nor forsake us. He promises. If your husband leaves you, God will not. If your friends fall away, God will not. If your hope fades, God will not. If your dreams crumble, God will not. Listen to His gentle voice full of unwavering faithfulness: "I will never leave you nor forsake you."

But if God hasn't left me, then why are bad things still happening? This is a hard truth, but it must be learned. Remember those Camp Wilderness lessons? It's time to learn one.

God allows bad things to happen.

God allows earthquakes to hit. God allows famine to strike poverty-stricken nations. God allows cancer to take lives. And God allows the free will of man.

From the very beginning of creation, God gave Adam and Eve the gift of free will. He didn't create them as puppets, bowing to His every whim. He created them as individual, thinking, choosing, human beings. When God created man, He gave him the freedom to choose. God set up boundaries and gave guidelines, and then He gave Adam and Eve the freedom to choose whether or not to follow them.

And as painful as it seems, God gave your spouse the freedom to choose as well. Your husband is allowed the choice to be faithful or to stray. He is allowed the choice to be honorable or despicable. He is allowed the choice to obey God or to disobey. God will not force His will on anyone. That is not how He created us—it's not part of the original design.

Because of the sin of man, we live on an imperfect

planet. And until we get to heaven, tsunamis will obliterate shores, disease will ravage nations, civil wars will destroy populations, and mankind will operate in the freedom to choose right or wrong.

Well, that's depressing! Kinda. But take another step back, and realize a second truth. Even though God allows bad stuff to happen, it doesn't mean that He is not at work. In fact, that is one of the most wonderful things about God. In the midst of the maelstrom of life, in the very heart of the turmoil, across the eons of civilizations and even galaxies—God is constantly, unfailingly, and perfectly at work. And although He is deeply saddened, His throne room is not rocked, and His plans are not thwarted when your husband walks out on your marriage.

*I am the LORD, and there is no other; apart from me there is no God.* Isaiah 45:5

In Chapter 45 of Isaiah, God says five different times that He is God and there is no other God. "I will go before you and will level the mountains... It is I who made the earth and created mankind upon it. My own hands have stretched out the heavens; I marshaled their starry hosts... I summon you by name and bestow on you a title of honor... I will strengthen you... I form the light and create darkness." I encourage you to read the entire chapter—it's an uplifting reminder of the power of God.

So God allows bad things to happen, but He is still in charge. How does that help me in my life down here on earth? Well, the final part of this equation is the best part! When awful things happen, not only are they not outside God's power, but He is often using them to bring about a much greater good. Now, I know what you're thinking (because I thought the same thing). That sounds like one of those trite placations people offer when they don't know what to say. "It'll all work out for the good, you'll see." Really? How could my husband leaving me with a baby, a thousand miles from my family, and with no way to support myself be a good thing?! How exactly does that work out for this touchy-feely, universal "greater good"?

Because our Heavenly Father is a good God. And He is a God who loves us. He loves you.

*And we know that in all things God works for the good of those who love him, who have been called according to his purpose.* Romans 8:28

God is actively at work in your situation. And He is doing a good work for you. Because He loves you.

In the midst of your grief, God is loving you. You may not be able to see or feel it, but He is loving you this very moment. He has not forgotten you. Not at all. Remember, He is trying to teach you. He is trying to mold you into an amazing person. All because He loves you.

*'For I know the plans I have for you,' declares the LORD,*
*'Plans to prosper you and not to harm you, plans to give*
*you a hope and a future.' Jeremiah 29:11*

Did you catch that? Not only does God love you, He has a plan for you. And not only does He have a plan, but it's a good plan! It's a plan to prosper you! A plan to give you a hope and a future! I know it may not seem like it, I know it's hard to even think about it, but you have hope. You have a future—and it's a really good one.

It doesn't matter right now what it is. You don't have to process the concept of your future any more than just knowing God is holding it in His hands. Surrender your hope and future to Him who sits on the throne. In your darkest hour, God is at work. He is still on the throne, He loves you, and He has a plan to prosper you—to give you a hope and a future. Hallelujah!

*See Appendix for all five locations

## Chapter 6

# NO OTHER GODS

"**D**o you love me, Suzanne?"
Of course I love you Lord.
"Do you really love me, Suzanne?"
Maybe you didn't hear me. Of course I do.
"But do you really love me, Suzanne?"
Um, did you not hear me the first two times? I said yes, I love you, Lord!

And I did love God. I really did. But if I was honest with myself, I didn't love God with all my heart. I loved Him with most of it, but not all of it. I was holding back a little bit. When I sang songs about God being my all in all, I meant it. But I was deceiving myself. And it wasn't until Phil left me that I realized it.

As wives, we are called to love and honor our husbands. It's part of the whole marriage thing. Be his helpmate, his champion, and his lover. And as I said my vows, I couldn't wait to love my husband in every way that God intended. Our marriage was going to be everything God designed marriage to be, the marriage of all marriages! Cue the triumphant music.

But somewhere along the way, I became enraptured with my husband. And while this is not necessarily a bad thing, I spent more time thinking about and loving my husband than I did thinking about and loving God.

As a wife, it's hard straddling the two worlds of the physical and spiritual. Our husbands need us to iron their shirts, our boss needs the proposal by noon, our kids need us to make their lunch, and the dog needs to go out. But God also calls us to spend time at His feet. It is hard to be all things to all needers. Libraries are filled with books on how to make it all work in the modern woman's world.

And I thought I was doing a pretty good job at keeping all the plates spinning. We enjoyed our adult Sunday school class, Phil helped lead worship in church, I was moving up the management chain at work, and I occasionally squeezed in a Bible study. Heck, I even played on the church softball team. Pretty darn holy, huh? (Second base and catcher for those who want to know.)

"Suzanne, do you love me?"

Is that you again? Didn't you hear me singing with gusto in the pew yesterday?

"But do you really love me?"

Hello, I made it to Bible study on Tuesday, and even got most of my lesson done.

"That's good—I hope you learned something helpful. But do you love me?"

God, you know my heart. You should know how much I love you. Why do you keep bugging me?

Silence.

For God did indeed know my heart. Of course He did. He knew my heart so much better than I did. And He knew that I wasn't loving Him with all of it. I was loving my husband instead.

*You shall have no other gods before me.* Exodus 20:3

Well duh, God. I know that. It was you I was worshiping at church, remember?

"Who did you spend the rest of your time longing for?"

*You shall not make for yourself an idol in the form of anything in heaven above or on earth below. You shall not bow down to them or worship them.* Exodus 20:4-5a

Now that's just weird, Lord. I don't have any Buddha statues around the house, and I'm not crafting anything in my idol workshop out back.

Tragedy has a way of distilling truth. The foggy becomes clear, and fallacies neatly buried are catapulted to the surface. The thought of my husband leaving was so incomprehensible. It was paralyzing and devastating

37

to me. Because, somewhere along the way, I started loving Phil more than I loved God.

*Love the LORD your God with all your heart and with all your soul and with all your strength.* Deuteronomy 6:5

When I was in college, I volunteered to be a guinea pig for an advanced Psychology class. They were doing personality diagnostics as part of their graduation requirements and needed test subjects. I love that kind of stuff, so I was an eager participant.

The tests took a couple of hours and covered a wide range of cognitive thinking processes. I flipped and rotated shapes in my mind, connected dots, described images, and completed story lines. I was really enjoying the whole process, and then I was shown a picture. It was a drawing of a woman looking at a door with a somewhat neutral, if not slightly sad, expression. The proctor asked me to describe what was happening.

To my surprise, I burst into tears and described a story where the woman's husband was away at war, and she was longing for his return. But, she knew deep in her heart that he was never coming back. Wow! Where did that come from? I looked up at the grad student in a bit of shock, and she did her best to keep a passive face as she scribbled notes.

My own father is a wonderful man who loved my

mom faithfully—they're still happily married today. I had never experienced a painful loss like the one I described in the drawing at all. My final year at college was filled with gleeful wedding plans. I didn't know where my deep-seated fear of losing my husband had been planted. But obviously it was there.

Was that a spiritual warning to me about my future? Maybe. It was eye-opening to me, but I wasn't sure what, if anything, to do about it. So I just filed it away in my brain.

When Phil walked out the door, the image of the forlorn woman watching at the door and all my emotions about her came rushing back. Only this time, the woman wasn't just a drawing; she was me. And I was living the nightmare I had described so many years before.

Everything I knew, or thought I knew, about love had been destroyed. My house of love was razed to the ground. When the dust cleared, and the truth revealed, I did the only thing I could: I fell at the feet of my Father.

I began to learn to deeply and passionately love the One who would never leave me. I began to love, above all else, the One who created me and has good plans for me. In the rubble of my life, I put God back where He belonged: first place in my life. I was clinging to the fact that He loved me. Now, it was time for me to learn how to love Him in return.

*...God is love. Whoever lives in love lives in God, and God in him. We love because he first loved us.* 1 John 4:16b, 19

Examine your life closely, my sister. If God is not your number one focus, He needs to be. He longs for your love. Maybe, through your divorce, He is revealing any obstacles that have been distracting you from Him. It was not a fun process for me, but oh the freedom in loving God above all else! When I chose to place God at the top of my priority list, I could feel all the pieces of my life starting to right themselves. Place your love in the One who will cherish it, protect it, and honor it. Love the Lord your God with all your heart, with all your soul, and with all your strength—and let the healing begin!

## Chapter 7

# PRAISE HIM IN THE STORM

Storms are part of the human existence—both in weather and in life. We all know someone who has experienced more than their fair share of sorrow. And I don't think any of us believe that we will get through life without any wounds. But what separates you from anyone else, what makes your own personal tragedy unique, is not the event itself, but how you respond to it.

The story of Horatio Spafford makes me cry every time I hear it. Mr. Spafford was a wealthy American during the mid-1800s who sent his wife and four young daughters to England on holiday. He planned to follow later. As they crossed the Atlantic Ocean, their steamship was struck by another vessel. Two hundred and twenty-six people were lost in the cold waters. His wife survived—but his daughters did not. When she reached England, she sent her husband a telegram saying, "Saved Alone."

I cannot imagine the death of my child, much less the death of four daughters. His grief must have been overwhelming. But somehow, by strength drawn only from walking with God through the darkest places, Horatio Spafford chose to praise the Lord. How do we know? As he crossed the Atlantic on the same route where his daughters perished, he wrote one of the church's most treasured hymns. And whether or not you're familiar with the tune, the words say it all:

*"When peace, like a river, attendeth my way,*

*When sorrows like sea billows roll;*

*Whatever my lot, Thou hast taught me to say,*

*It is well, it is well with my soul."*

How does someone do that? How does a man consumed by grief write a song, not about tragedy, but about peace? About how his soul is well. The answer lies not in the man himself, but in the God he served. Horatio Spafford was acting in obedience to God.

*Consider it pure joy, my brothers, whenever you face trials of many kinds...* James 1:2

Are you kidding me? Consider it pure joy when I face a trial? Right. That sounds like some sadistic teaching that ancient monks who whip themselves would follow. Why on earth would I consider my divorce pure joy? James goes on to say:

*...because you know that the testing of your faith
develops perseverance. Perseverance must finish its work
so that you may be mature and complete, not lacking
anything.* James 1:3-4

What if I don't want to be mature and complete? I can smile about it now, but there were many times when I thought that if this was the path to maturity and wisdom, then I don't want them! I was happier in my ignorant immaturity. But God wanted more from me. God was giving me the chance to grow in my faith, the chance to move from a so-so spirituality to a place of blessing and fulfillment. He is giving you the same chance.

I couldn't ignore those yucky verses in James. "Consider it pure joy." It doesn't say to feel deep joy or act joyful. It just says to consider it pure joy. Out of sheer obedience, and nothing else, I began, ever so slowly, to consider the trials I was experiencing as pure joy.

It was really hard at first. I felt that by praising God, I was somehow saying that what I was going through wasn't painful and didn't really matter. Which of course, wasn't true. But the more I got on my knees to consider my trials pure joy, the more I realized that God was waiting to bless me in the midst of my storm.

*These (trials) have come so that your faith—of greater
worth than gold, which perishes even though refined by
fire—may be proved genuine and may result in praise,
glory and honor when Jesus Christ is revealed.* 1 Peter 1:7

43

My faith was being refined, my faith was being proved genuine, and my faith will result in praise, glory, and honor when Jesus is revealed. Pretty heady stuff. God is giving you the same chance, the same opportunity. That's all storms really are: opportunities for our faith to grow, opportunities for us to move beyond the basics and enjoy a relationship with our Father that belongs only to those who bear scars.

*Dear friends, do not be surprised at the painful trial you are suffering, as though something strange were happening to you. But rejoice that you participate in the sufferings of Christ, so that you may be overjoyed when his glory is revealed. 1 Peter 3:13*

I once heard a powerful sermon about the trials Christ went through on His way to the cross. The physical and emotional suffering was horrible. But then, the preacher turned it on us. He said that as followers of Christ, why wouldn't we expect to suffer as well? Sometimes Christians think that because they are worshiping God, nothing bad will happen to them. But, this preacher was saying the opposite. Not only did Christ suffer, but you, as His followers, will suffer as well. Um, I don't think I meant to sign up for that part...

*So then, those who suffer according to God's will should commit themselves to their faithful Creator and continue to do good. 1 Peter 4:19*

What is it with Peter and his suffering theme? Maybe he experienced it first-hand. Legend says that Peter was later crucified—upside down—for spreading the gospel of Jesus Christ. Whether or not this was true, no doubt he was persecuted for his faith. No doubt Peter knew what it was to suffer.

\*\*\*

Fierce storms blow up on the Sea of Galilee, often with very little warning. One day, as the disciples are traveling across the sea, they are hit by such a storm.\* The Bible says that their boat was in danger of being swamped. They are doing everything they can to keep their little craft afloat, and where is Jesus? Bailing water with them and helping to toss over any extra weight? Or maybe He is manning an oar with super human strength? No, Jesus isn't doing anything to help keep the boat from sinking. In fact, during this furious storm, Jesus is sleeping. Now that's tired! The disciples wake Him up, and He commands the wind and the storm to be still. And it does. Then He reprimands them for their lack of faith.

Cool story. But one of my favorite details that often gets overlooked is the location of Jesus. Where was He in the midst of the terrifying storm? Jesus wasn't on land calling out orders to them, telling them to paddle faster, He wasn't high on a hill waving torches in the

Christian Chick's Guide to Surviving Divorce

direction they should go, and He wasn't floating above them watching them suffer. Jesus was in the boat, right in the middle of the storm, with the disciples He loved.

And there, riding out the storm with you in your boat, is Jesus. Call on Him. He may decide to calm the storm for you, or He may simply choose to calm you instead. But either way, He is with you in your storm. He is in your boat.

And finally, one last storm story. The disciples are back at it again on the Sea of Galilee when another storm blows up. You'd think they would have learned their lesson or at least gotten a better forecaster. But this time, Jesus sends them on ahead of Him, and once again, the wind and waves threaten to sink their boat.** The terrified disciples do everything they can to keep from drowning, and then they look up and see Jesus walking towards them on the water.

Peter tells Jesus he wants to walk on the water out to Him; Jesus invites him to do so. And for a bit, Peter walks on the water as well. But then, Peter looks around and sees the wind and waves. He is terrified and begins to sink, but Jesus immediately reaches out and grabs him. Then they both climb into the boat.

Jesus walking on the water during a major storm is pretty cool, but don't miss another important point. While Peter kept his eyes on Jesus, he was able to walk on water. But the minute he took his eyes off the Lord and focused on the storm, Peter sank.

46

Are you sinking in your storm right now? Are the waves of pain and despair threatening to swamp your little boat? When the thunder shakes your very core and the wind threatens to rip you apart, it is not easy to focus on Jesus. But you must. Instead of keeping your eyes on the howling storm, your court order, your bills, your breaking heart, you must keep them on the One who walks across the water with arms outstretched, to you.

But how? How do you keep going? How do you not just keep your head above the water, but walk on it? By praising God. Praising God during a trial strengthens your faith, but it also helps you to take your eyes off the trial and put them back on God. Being in the midst of a bad situation can be all-consuming. You lose sleep, and concentrating on anything else important is difficult at best. But take a lesson from Peter, and focus your attention not on the storm itself, but on the One who has the power to calm the storm.

One last bit of encouragement from this story. What happens when Peter's faith falters and he begins to sink? Jesus immediately reaches out and grabs Him. He lifts Peter out of the water, and they climb safely back into the boat. And Jesus does the same for you. If your faith is faltering and you feel yourself slipping under the cold water, look for the hand of Jesus. He will not let you drown. Jesus wants you to keep your eyes on Him, but when your strength is gone, He will reach out, lift you up, and save you from the storm.

This divorce you are experiencing is a chance for your faith to be refined. It's a chance for God's glory to be revealed, and it's a chance for you to grow in maturity and wisdom. Don't miss this chance. Praise God in the midst of your divorce. Out of sheer obedience, when you can't even think straight, praise God. The Bible tells us that when we praise the name of God, Satan must flee. Send Satan and his demons running. Choose to praise the Lord.

*And the God of all grace, who called you to his eternal glory in Christ, after you have suffered a little while, will himself restore you and make you strong, firm and steadfast. 1 Peter 5:10*

Oh my suffering friend, let the Lord restore you and make you strong, firm, and steadfast. Choose the path to life, healing, and hope. Praise Him. Praise Him in the storm. Praise Him in your divorce.

*Mark 4:35-44
**Matthew 14:22-33

Chapter 8

# WHO ARE WE FIGHTING ANYWAY?

I was angry. Angry and hurt and panicking. Phil had found a "special friend" at work and was spending a lot of time with her. I'll call her Amanda. I brought up my concerns about her with Phil, but he brushed them aside. I was overreacting. Amanda was just a co-worker, that was all. There was nothing going on between them. And maybe that was true—at least at the beginning.

But then, concerned friends started telling me about incidents they witnessed. A fellow co-worker happened upon them "flirting" in a stairwell. Maybe out of compassion, she spared me the details. Another friend saw my husband having lunch with Amanda at an outdoor restaurant in our town, and the conversation seemed quite intimate.

I had met Amanda a couple of times before. She was pretty and vivacious, and single. She knew that Phil and I were expecting our first child. Friends advised me to show up at Phil's office from time to time and see if he wanted to go to lunch—just to remind everyone (Amanda) that I existed. So I tried that a couple of times. I'd bring in cookies and say hi to the whole gang. And after Molly was born, I'd stop by to show her off. Everyone at Phil's office would coo and pass Molly around, but I felt their pity, and knew when I left, the gossip would start again. I felt like a fool.

What I really wanted to do was barge in there and scream at her and say something like: "Look at me, you witch (PG version in total disclosure.) Phil has a wife, and it's me! We have a baby—a newborn, for Pete's sake. Are you out of your mind? Are you trying to destroy our marriage?! Because it's working. And then what will you get? Your prize will be a man who is willing to cheat on his pregnant wife. Now there's something worth stealing."

I don't understand what makes one woman entice another woman's husband. As women, we know how deeply we feel things. We understand how much it means to have a man who loves you, who will be faithful to you. And yet, every day, the other woman is out there lurking, just waiting for the right timing. In my darker moments, I wished that one day another woman would do the same thing to Amanda that she did to me. Not proud of that, but that's how I felt.

Relatively soon after our divorce, Amanda moved across the country. I think they've stayed in touch, but she and Phil never got together. Which, in a weird twisted way, made me even madder. *So you help destroy my marriage, and then you don't even hook up with my husband? The prize you so cunningly hunted? You got what you wanted—my husband left me. And now, you up and leave? Was this all just a game to you?! Because it sure wasn't a game to me. My life is utterly destroyed because of what you have done. I am now a single mother with a baby, and she will never know what it's like to have her mother and father in the same house. Is that what you wanted? Because that's the result of your "playful fling!"* Last I heard, Amanda has a baby now herself, but never married.

I was angry at Amanda. But, if I was honest with myself, I knew that Amanda was really just one part of the crumbling marriage equation. It wasn't really about Amanda at all. She just happened to be the one to stumble across my husband's path when he was looking for a distraction.

So, if Amanda wasn't the root of the problem, I needed to go to the source: Phil. Our divorce was Phil's fault. Put the blame where blame is due. After all, what kind of man begins an inappropriate relationship with another woman while his own wife is pregnant?

It's easy to judge people by their behavior. But for

every behavior, good or bad, there is always a why. The same was true for Phil. Phil's parents have always had a dysfunctional marriage. And on one side, Phil's grandparents had a dysfunctional relationship. So, growing up, Phil didn't have a good example of what a marriage should be. He never told me exactly why, but regarding his family, there always seemed to be deep-seated anger and resentment.

Phil's mother and I are as different as night and day. We used to laugh about how her house was always spotless, and mine was always happy chaos. She was an excellent cook, and I was really good at going out to eat. She valued rules, order, and the system, while I craved expression, freedom, and broke rules from time to time just for the fun of it. Neither one of these personalities are wrong. But, they created a stark contrast between the home in which Phil grew up and the home he shared with his wife. These differences went from amusing, to annoying, and eventually for Phil, to deal-breaking.

I don't know when it was, but one day, Phil didn't want to try anymore. He was unhappy, and he didn't want to make our marriage work. I was willing to work on our issues. I tried cooking, with moderate success. I tried keeping the house cleaner—I even organized the spice shelf alphabetically. I wanted to hear what was bothering him and work on it, but Phil was already done. He wasn't interested in talking, listening, or working on our marriage.

That made me mad.

No marriage is perfect. Marriages require work. I was not perfect, but I was willing to work on my flaws. Phil was not, and I couldn't make him. I couldn't make him want to try, I couldn't make him love me, and I couldn't keep him from walking out the door.

So, I had some catty conversations bashing Amanda, the other woman. I enjoyed some judgmental moments shaking my head at how Phil's dysfunctional family had contributed to our marriage's collapse. I owned the faults that were truly mine, and then I dumped the rest of it on Phil. I placed the failure of our marriage on him. I blamed him for not dealing with the issues in his past before we committed to marriage, I blamed him for marrying me, and then trying to change me, and I blamed him for seeking out Amanda's company instead of mine.

Who are you blaming for the failure of your marriage? Is there an Amanda in your husband's life? Perhaps it's not another woman, but an unhealthy relationship nonetheless. Is your husband drunk more than sober, with every event centering around his next drink? Does your bank account dwindle on payday while he spends his nights at Off-Track Betting? Or maybe you found rampant pornography hidden on his computer or under the mattress, demanding that you compete with women who don't exist. Who, or what, is at fault for your divorce? Perhaps your husband loves his job more than you, giving all his attention to his corporate mistress? Maybe there were skeletons that came out of the closet right after the honeymoon. Or did you marry a fixer-upper, knowing there were major issues, but feeling confident you could correct them?

Oh the blame! In the midst of my swirling grief, I will, rather ashamedly, admit to the small twisted pleasure of blaming all the other sinners who contributed to my failed marriage. My girlfriends would validate my ranting, and I'd feel slightly better. And then one day, I came across a scripture verse that rocked my world.

*For our struggle is not against flesh and blood, but against the rulers, against the authorities, against the powers of this dark world and against the spiritual forces of evil in the heavenly realms.* Ephesians 6:12

"For our struggle is not against flesh and blood." What does that mean, my struggle is not against flesh and blood? Of course it is. I married a flesh and blood husband. It was his flesh and blood that lied to me about hitting a club with Amanda last night. What on earth is that verse talking about?

Here is another life lesson to be learned: what happens on earth is merely a reflection of what is going on in the spiritual realm. "Whoa!" you say, "The spiritual realm? Now you're getting all weird on me." Stay with me. I promise it will make sense.

Almost everyone, with the exception of the most hardened heart, agrees that we are spiritual beings. All over the earth, mankind practices spirituality. From the most primitive tribes worshiping the jungle jinn to the parishioners at the cathedral of Notre Dame, the human race is a spiritual race.

And, no matter their religion, people know there is a difference between good and bad, right and wrong. There is an innate knowledge of morality among mankind. Sometimes it is corrupted by evil regimes and ancient customs, or selfish motives, greed, and power. But the vast majority of people, no matter their race or level of education, know that it is wrong to steal from a blind person or to rape an innocent child.

Why do they know this? Because humans are born with a knowledge of right and wrong. Innate spirituality if you will. We are spiritual beings living in a spiritual world with two forces at play: good and evil.

Now obviously, the author of all things good is God, and it follows that Satan is the holder of all things evil. But, there are many other forces at work underneath God and Satan. Both God and Satan have armies that do their bidding and both have far-reaching spiritual warriors and messengers who are allowed to interact with humans here on earth: angels and demons.

I want to make it clear that I don't think Phil was ever demon-possessed at all. But I do think he allowed the seeds of doubt to be planted. He allowed himself to be swayed by lies. And he allowed himself to entertain temptation.

"Your wife will never understand you or appreciate you," Satan might hiss. Or, "You don't really want to spend the rest of your life being unhappy with the woman you married, do you?" And, "You deserve to have what you want. Life is too short to throw it away on a nagging woman!"

Our struggle is not against flesh and blood.

But what about all that baggage he brought into our marriage, Lord? What about Amanda? Surely those factors contributed to our divorce. Didn't they Lord?

Phil has two siblings who grew up in the same family as he did—and they're both happily married with beautiful stable families. Attractive women work in offices all over the world, and the vast majority of them are not home-wreckers. Circumstances can affect and even contribute to behavior, but ultimately, people make choices. Choices to be faithful, or to betray, choices to rise above their past, or succumb to it.

I had made a fatal error. While I was desperately trying to keep Amanda away from my husband, and trying to psychoanalyze his upbringing, Satan was attacking Phil through the back door.

For our struggle is not against flesh and blood.

I was fighting the wrong enemy. Phil wasn't my

enemy, his family history wasn't my enemy, and as hard as it was to let it go, Amanda wasn't my enemy either. My enemy dwelt in the spiritual realm. My battle was "against the powers of this dark world and against the spiritual forces of evil in the heavenly realms."

Marriage, since it is a God-ordained structure, threatens Satan. The very existence of a healthy marriage can bring about generations of healthy families—all in defiance of Satan's plans. And a strong Christian marriage is one of Satan's worst nightmares. He will do everything in his power to attack and destroy it. He doesn't fight fair, and nothing is off-limits for him. Not your bank account, not your home, not your job, not your spouse, and not your children.

So it's okay to be angry with your husband. It's okay to blame the other woman, the alcohol, the job, the porn. But know that those are just symptoms of Satan at work. He or his demons placed those temptations in front of your husband when your mate was at his weakest, because that is what he does.

But don't give up—it's gets a whole lot better, I promise. Keep reading!

\*\*\*

By now, if you're not used to thinking about events on earth also taking place in the spiritual realm, you're probably a little freaked out. What are we supposed to do? Are there angels and demons in this very room with me? Is Satan lurking in my front bushes waiting to ambush me?

Fortunately for us, Paul tells us who we are fighting—the spiritual forces of evil—and then he tells us how to fight. The very next verse in Ephesians offers instructions.

*Therefore put on the full armor of God, so that when the day of evil comes, you may be able to stand your ground, and after you have done everything, to stand.* Ephesians 6:13

Put on the full armor of God? What is that? Well, I'm glad you asked, because Paul explains what the armor is in the next set of verses.

*Stand firm then, with the belt of truth buckled around your waist, with the breastplate of righteousness in place, and with your feet fitted with the readiness that comes from the gospel of peace. In addition to all this, take up the shield of faith, with which you can extinguish all the flaming arrows of the evil one. Take the helmet of salvation and the sword of the Spirit, which is the word of God.* Ephesians 6:13-17

Aren't those verses cool? I imagine a mighty warrior dressing for battle. Perhaps the sun is just coming up over the hill. After one final check of his armor, he is ready for the fight. He grabs his sword and walks out to face his enemy.

Entire Bible studies have been written detailing these verses about the armor of God, and I encourage you to do more research on them when you are ready. But in the meantime, all you really need to know is that, even though our battle is not against flesh and blood, God has given you all the weapons you will ever need to fight in the spiritual realm. Most of these weapons are defensive: the breastplate of righteousness and the shield of faith. And some are offensive: shoes fitted with readiness and the sword of the Spirit. If you are trusting in the salvation of God, then these weapons belong to you.

Even if the battle for your marriage is lost, Satan will continue to attack you. He wants you to be a fragile shell of your former self. He cannot afford for you to come back stronger than before. But that, my friend, is exactly what God has in mind for you: to rise from the ashes of your marriage. Wounded and scarred, but wiser in the knowledge of who the real enemy is.

Sometimes I imagine myself putting on each piece of God's armor. On the really bad days when I feel under heavy attack, I'll say it out loud, "I am buckling on the belt of truth." And then I speak out loud the things I know to be true: "I am a child of God. God loves me. God has plans to prosper me and not to harm me. God will never leave me nor forsake me." And then, I proceed through each piece of armor, visualizing myself putting it on and speaking aloud what it will do for me. Try this yourself. Whether you wanted this fight or not, you have been called to be a warrior. Fight for your children if you have them. And fight for yourself. Satan may celebrate the destruction of your marriage, but don't let him celebrate the destruction of you.

One final thought on spiritual battles: ultimately this is not our fight. When it's all said and done, we are merely whispers in the annals of time. While we are indeed called to be warriors for the days we spend on earth, ours is not the final fight for the heavenly realm. Ours is the fight for obedience to a Father who loves us. Ours is the fight against the evil forces during our temporal existence. But ultimately, this battle is between good and evil—between Satan and God Himself.

And if you look at the end of the book, God wins. Rest in that knowledge today, dear friend. If your sword feels heavy and your shield feels tattered, run back to your Father's arms of safety.

*For the battle is not yours, but God's...You will not have to fight this battle. Take up your positions; stand firm and see the deliverance the LORD will give you.* 2 Chronicles 20:15b, 17a

I wish I could tell you that the Amandas will go away now that you know who the real enemy is. But they won't. I want to be able to assure you that past dysfunction and current temptations will no longer influence your marriage, and the forces that seek to destroy your relationship will fade away. But I can't tell you that, because they won't. They will continue to attack you, your husband, and your marriage. I can't promise that God will save your marriage. But, at least now you know who you're fighting, and you know how to do it.

Show up at the fight, dressed for battle and prepared. Stand firm in your armor. But do not be afraid; do not be discouraged. For the battle belongs to the Lord. Tighten up that helmet and shield, and draw your sword. Stand firm and see the deliverance the Lord will give you!

## Chapter 9

# HUMILIATION HOEDOWN

Divorce is humiliating! Your private pain is thrust in front of your family, your friends, and anyone else who might be interested. And they're all interested— some because they can't wait to shake their heads and say they knew it was coming, some because it makes them feel better about their own marriage. "Well at least my husband didn't leave me for the tramp down the street." And some because they need a new gossip subject. "Did you hear about Suzanne? Her husband is divorcing her. Poor thing. She seemed like she had it all together. Obviously, there were issues." They wink knowingly.

At the very core, you feel like you chose the wrong guy. You made a mistake way back then, and now you're paying for it. If you'd just been a little smarter or wiser, waited longer, read the tea leaves, listened to your mother, or never gotten married in the first place, none of this would have happened. Clearly you were a fool for marrying him. How could you be so stupid?

It's humiliating when your neighbors tell you, after the fact, about the strange car in your driveway while you were out of town. How long have they been watching out their windows, and what else have they seen? It's humiliating when the bank officer turns down your loan because your husband's credit score is in the toilet due to his secret habit that evidently you should have known about. All the tellers at the bank certainly did. Or maybe you contributed to your divorce. Maybe you behaved less than honorably, and everyone knows it. Humiliating.

It's hard when all of your friends are going to the couple's retreat for the weekend, and suddenly you're not a couple anymore. Does that mean you are not invited? Who do you even ask to see if you can go, and do you really want to anyway? It's humiliating dropping your child off at the church nursery when you're not wearing a wedding ring, or when the singles class at your church is full of gray-haired widows who look at you like you don't belong. And they're right.

It was so humiliating for me to have to check the "divorced" box when I updated my information in the church directory. And the absolute worst was when I filled out a job application at a local Christian college and had to explain, in detail, why I was divorced. Could you just kick me while I'm already lying in the dirt?

Out in the "real world" divorce doesn't have the stigma it used to. Everybody's doing it. We all know the statistic that about half of all marriages end in divorce. *Oh great, now I'm part of that awful statistic too.* Everyone knows someone, or married someone, or is someone who got a divorce. We're all one big sad, unfortunate, pathetic, happy family. A gross generalization to be sure. But it was still a group I never planned on being identified with.

It was hard for me when the news trickled back to my childhood home, when my parents' friends and long-time friends of the family started finding out. They were gracious and compassionate, but I was still ashamed. And what do you say at your ten-year high school reunion when everyone has a great job and two precious kids with another on the way? "Here is my adorable little girl, and my husband is leaving me. She'll always be an only child, and I have no idea how I'm going to support myself." That's a bit of a downer.

Depressing! I finally had to decide not to dwell on all that stuff because it was threatening to suck me into a pit of self-despair out of which I could never crawl. *God, I feel like I am worthless. Please help me to feel your love. I feel like I'm condemned to that section of pews where all the people of questionable morality sit. I feel so humiliated. Please help me to not be ashamed.*

*Therefore, there is no condemnation for those who are in Christ Jesus.* Romans.

Did you catch that? Read that verse again. "There

is no condemnation for those who are in Christ Jesus." God is not condemning you. Who cares what the nursery worker thinks? Did you make mistakes? There is no condemnation. Your neighbor's opinion isn't all that important in the larger scheme of life. Are you embarrassed? God is not condemning you. There is no condemnation for those who are in Christ Jesus. It doesn't say there is no condemnation for those who are blameless, and it doesn't say it for those who have it all together. The only requirement is to be in Christ Jesus. Walk in the freedom of that today, sweet sister. When Satan feeds you lies and makes you feel worthless, speak aloud what you know to be true. "Therefore, there is no condemnation for those who are in Christ Jesus."

***

It is important to recognize the difference between humility and being humiliated. Godly humility is a character trait. Humility is an attribute highly esteemed by God and has nothing to do with being embarrassed or ashamed. Shame and guilt are the flip-side, impostor characteristics that Satan wants you to take on. So how do we attain humility without believing Satan's lies of worthlessness?

*Humble yourself before the Lord, and he will lift you up.*
James 4:10

There is so much wisdom and power in this little verse. First of all, who is doing the humbling here? You are. Before I went through my divorce, I thought I had a pretty decent grasp on humility. I recognized that the talents I had were from God, and I needed to follow His plan if I wanted to be blessed and get the most out of my life. I laugh now. I had NO idea what humility felt like.

God is giving you the chance to humble yourself. Not very hard when you're in the midst of a divorce. I have never felt more humble than when my husband didn't want me anymore, my future was completely unknown, and I was standing in front of a judge who was about to dictate to me my net worth and how I was going to live my life. Pretty humbling. God will allow you to be placed in humbling circumstances, but He gives you the chance to humble yourself first. Try that route. It's a lot easier, trust me.

"Humble yourself before the Lord, and He will lift you up." Don't miss the second part of this verse. It's the best part. Once you humble yourself, it will be your Heavenly Father lifting you back up again. God is not a crusher of dreams, He doesn't hold grudges, and He's not waiting for you to screw up so He can bash you. On the contrary, God wants to lift you up. He's waiting for you. Will you let Him be the lifter of your head?

I remember a couple of instances, not big, earth-shattering moments, but instances nonetheless where

I felt God lifting my head. One time, a dear friend encouraged me to audition for a local production of *Peter Pan*. At the time, Phil and I were separated and in that fragile no-man's land of *where is this marriage headed?* My self-confidence was not in tip-top shape, so I hesitated, but decided to try out anyway. I won one of the lead roles: Tiger Lily. For the next several months, I got to act on stage, dance my heart out, and wear a beautiful costume. It was a life's breath of joy for me in my world of turmoil. I felt pretty, and special, and appreciated. All temporal to be sure, but exactly what I needed at that time in my life. A little lifting of my head from the Lord.

And then one day I was flying back to Chicago after visiting my family in Dallas. It was always so hard to leave them and come back to my husband who didn't want me. I was on the plane when this lovely woman stopped me and asked if I was a Luvabull—a professional cheerleader for the Chicago Bulls. She seemed shocked when I said no. Now, if you know anything about professional cheerleading, you know that you need to be at least 5'6". I'm five feet flat with my cute shoes on. But just the fact that a total stranger would even think that I resembled a Luvabull was enough to cheer me on for weeks. God bless that woman! I hope we'll meet in heaven one day so I can tell her what an encouragement her innocent question was.

You may have never wanted to be Tiger Lily and wouldn't be caught dead shaking your pompons wearing spandex in public, but I bet the Lord is just waiting to be the lifter of your head. Don't despair, sweet friend. God has not forgotten you. He has seen your humiliation and will pick you up and dust you off. You never know when or where He'll surprise you.

∗∗∗

*The sacrifices of God are a broken spirit; a broken and contrite heart, O God, you will not despise.* Psalms 51:17

Oh, I was broken. In the depths of my grief, I recounted every sin I'd ever done. I was sorry for every time I'd been mouthy to my mom and for sneaking in way past my curfew in high school. I acknowledged every moment of pride, every temptation that hooked me, and every fall I'd taken. I was so sorry. By that point, who was I trying to impress anymore? All I wanted was my husband back, and if that wasn't going to happen, I just wanted to be found righteous before the Lord. I had nothing else left.

Do you have a broken spirit and contrite heart? If so, you have great value before the Lord. Incidentally, these words in the Psalms were written by King David right after he was confronted about his adultery with

Bathsheba and the subsequent murder of her husband. Puts it all in perspective, huh? Your broken spirit is precious in the sight of God.

*The LORD is close to the brokenhearted and saves those who are crushed in spirit.* Psalms 34:18

Brokenhearted? Check. Crushed in spirit? Right here. King David is at it again, speaking God's truth from the depths of his own despair. Are you brokenhearted? God is near to you. And He's not just near, He's doing something about it. He's saving your crushed spirit. My spirit was a blithering, tear-covered, crumpled mess. And He saved me. He will save you too.

The Lord is close to you today, my friend. Don't waste these moments. In the midst of your despair, cry out to God. Humbling yourself (or God doing it for you) is not fun. But it is so very necessary for you to become the woman who God wants you to be. Throw away the shame, guilt, and humiliation. Replace them instead with godly humility, and let God be the lifter of your head. Blessings are just around the corner.

*Chapter 10*

# THE HONOR OF BEING CHOSEN

God will never give you more than you can handle. Do people tell you that? I hated that placation! Lord, I don't know who you think I am, but you must have me confused with someone else. Right now, I am so far underwater, I'm checking out Atlantis. I cannot do this, Father. I can't. I'm overwhelmed. I'm a single mother. My family is a thousand miles away. I don't know how to change the cord on the weed eater, and there are raccoons in my attic. Did I mention I have a baby? And I'm hurting. And I'm lonely. But I'm not supposed to freak out, because supposedly you will never give me more than I can handle. Well, I got news for you, God, this is way more than I can handle, and I'm freaking out!!

As much as I detested that phrase—God will never give you more than you can handle—it turned out to be true. However, it really needs an added prepositional phrase on the end (go ahead with the grammar geek jokes, I'm not fragile anymore.) God will never give you more than you can handle—with Him.

And that is the secret to it all. With the Lord at your side, you can get through anything. And I mean anything.

*Even though I walk through the valley of the shadow of death, I will fear no evil, for you are with me.* Psalms 23:4a

I have always loved this Psalm. Everyone does. But I don't think that until you've really walked through the valley, until you have tasted utter despair, and until you have been completely emptied out of yourself, you can truly understand this verse. Oh Father, my Shepherd, thank you that you walk through the valley of the shadow of death with me. Thank you that I am not alone in my journey.

I've mentioned it previously, but it bears repeating. Before my divorce, I was not a bad girl. I never sowed wild oats—I probably would have embarrassed myself if I had tried. I never played the prodigal. Now, there are a few episodes I'm not proud of, and some moments I hope my daughter doesn't ask me about one day. But overall, I was a solid Christian woman walking with the Lord.

And my story could have ended there. The world is full of stalwart Christians, walking with the Lord, who do great things for Him. Their story is pleasant, though unremarkable. And although I do not consider myself an unremarkable person, my spiritual journey was beginning to look that way.

Until God wanted more from me.

My spiritual ho-humness was okay with me, but it wasn't okay with God. He was about to allow my world to be completely rocked. He didn't cause my divorce, but He did allow it. God allowed Phil to divorce me— and this is a wild concept—because God decided I was worth the effort. "What on earth does that mean?" you ask.

It's kind of like taking swimming lessons when you're five, and the instructor is reaching out to you and motioning for you to come over. And, as a trusting student, you paddle enthusiastically towards her. Then, when you're almost there, gasping for breath, the teacher takes two steps backwards, forcing you to swim farther than you thought you could. I always hated when they did that! Just show me how far I have to swim, and I'll do it. None of this bait and switch game.

But, if God had shown me what my future had in store, not only would I have choked in the water, but I never would have gotten in the pool. *God, you've got the wrong girl! I think you've confused me with a different name on your cosmic Rolodex, maybe the one right before mine? Check again, Lord, because if you think I can get through this, you are out of your mind.* But of course, God didn't have me confused with someone else. He had me exactly where He wanted me.

*For you, O God, tested us;*
*you refined us like silver.* Psalms 66:10

The thing about the refiner's fire is...it's hot! Basic fire is hot, but the refiner's fire is scorching. It has to be extremely hot to burn off all the impurities. Wow, I must have had a lot of impurities. I always joked, "Why couldn't it be the refiner's bubble bath? Fire is so...hot. I'd like a softer method, please, Lord." That didn't happen. It's simply not possible to be refined in a bubble bath. Bummer.

And then there's that other fun analogy. The potter and the clay.

*Yet, O LORD, you are our Father. We are the clay, you are the potter; we are all the work of your hand.* Isaiah 64:8

Have you ever seen a master potter at work? It's pretty cool, but it's not a soft gentle process. In the beginning, the potter takes the lump of clay and beats the tar out of it. He pummels it and bashes it. Some potters even throw the lump against a wall. Why?

Because it gets rid of air bubbles. Air bubbles buried deep within clay are harmless when it is a wet lump. But when the pot has been shaped and is fired, air bubbles are fatal. The hidden bubbles weaken the structure of the entire piece, often rendering it unusable, suitable only for the trash pile.

*Does not the potter have the right to make out of the same lump of clay some pottery for noble purposes and some for common uses?* Romans 9:21

There's nothing wrong with a common pot. Some of them have important jobs to do. A chamber pot, for instance, is pretty darn important. But between you and me, I think I'd rather not be one. I'd like to be a chalice used for fine wine, or perhaps a decorative china vase residing in a palace. God wanted that for me. And He wants it for you.

Oh friend, your destiny is not that of a chamber pot. Your destiny is in the palace. How do I know? Because God chose you to experience His potter's wheel. We all experience pain in life. Some people lose their job, some get cancer, some lose a child. For you, one of these painful times is your divorce. God allowed your divorce to happen. He has chosen you for greater things. And you can choose to sit on His wheel while He shapes and molds you into something beautiful. It won't be easy, and at times it will be very painful. After all, the air bubbles must be beaten out, and the excess waste cut away. But, the end result will be a piece beyond price, chosen by God for greater things.

This whole divorce thing is not your final stop, you know. Although it may feel like it today, it's not. God is setting you up for those noble purposes talked about in the verse in Romans. You don't have to include Him in the process. You will survive this divorce and begin to heal one day, and you can hop off the potter's table yourself. We all know someone who has managed to get through their divorce without a deep faith. But who wants to do that? That's way too hard. Why would you want to try to put yourself back together when the Master Potter can do a far better job? It's kind of like trying to stitch yourself up after you accidentally cut yourself with a kitchen knife. You can probably do it, but that sounds really painful, and I'm thinking a doctor would be a much better bet. God knows what He is doing. Let Him do it. Stay on that potter's wheel and let Him finish the work He has started in you. If you let God continue to make you into something beautiful, you will be the vessel crafted by the Master.

*And we know that in all things God works for the good of those who love him, who have been called according to his purpose. Romans 8:28*

Remember that verse from our earlier chapter? God is calling you. He has a purpose for you, and He is working in your life. He is working for your good. This is not just an annoying saying to keep your head up. This is a promise in the Bible. In *all* things, God works for the good of those who love Him. In your divorce, right now, God is working for the good. When there are no answers and you just can't go another step, God is working for your good.

You are being called, my sister. Whether you wanted to be or not, whether you think God has the right name or not, you are being called. He is calling you because He wants more from you. He is calling you because you are worth the effort He is willing to make in molding and shaping you. He is calling you because He wants to work for good according to His purpose in your life. Although everyone goes through trials, not everyone will respond to God's call. Some will settle for life as a chamber pot. Don't let this be you. Your destiny is far greater. God is calling your name. You have the honor of being chosen.

## Chapter 11

# FORGIVENESS—THAT
# DIRTY WORD

If you saw this chapter heading in the Table of Contents, you might have been tempted to skip it. Maybe you did. Maybe you just glossed over these next two chapters and hoped I wouldn't notice. It's okay. I don't blame you. Forgiveness is a hard topic. You may have to read these two chapters several times before you're able to process the concepts. We are all works in progress—that's why it's called a journey, and not The End. I commend you that you're reading this at all. I promise you, you'll be glad you did, because this chapter is really about another "F" word. This is really a chapter about Freedom. Doesn't that sound a whole lot more fun than Forgiveness? Read on, dear friend. Take the first baby steps of forgiveness, and they will propel you towards freedom and the beginning of a new life. This time, it's all about you.

Nobody likes talking about forgiveness. If the subject comes up, it means that someone has been wronged or an injustice done. I don't know the circumstances of your divorce, but chances are you have been wronged by your mate somewhere along the way. And the odds are high, especially if you have children together, that you will continue to be wronged for a long time. Oh boy, oh boy. This sounds fun!

Divorced people can be an angry bunch. Have you noticed that? Therapy sessions can quickly deteriorate into furious rants and diatribes with venom spewing in all directions. Ranting can be helpful, and there is value in just getting it all out. But at some point, it's time to move on.

I am going to give you a dose of tough love here, my sister. Your friends love you and are trying to be supportive, so they are not going to tell you this. But I will. The ranting, angry phase is therapeutic and even fun for a bit, but you must move on. I'm telling you this because I want you to get your life back, and then live it. I am telling you this because I have been there. Lifelong anger is not your friend, nor is it your destiny.

You cannot stay angry forever. Well, that's not actually true. You can, but that initial righteous anger doesn't last. It morphs into bitterness, and bitterness is ugly. Have you seen that ugly, bitter woman recently? She's the one at the grocery store who slaps down the latest celebrity gossip magazine and says out loud to no one in particular: "Let's see what other gorgeous woman got left by her cheating husband." She looks up, hoping the clerk will comment, thus inviting a caustic speech about how all men should be castrated. The cashier is conveniently hard of hearing, and the rest of us try not to make eye contact. *I just want to buy my Diet Coke and pack of gum, lady.*

But you say, "I'm not bitter; I'm just hurt and angry." Okay, good. I'm going to help keep you from becoming the grocery store lady before it's too late. Remember, it's all about choosing life.

Do you ever notice that when you share a little bit of your story, other people try to top it? Everyone enjoys telling their own "done wrong" tale. Did your spouse lie about going away for the weekend? *Well my husband got a DUI while he was texting his mistress because he drove off the road and took down a gazebo. Yep, men are pigs. Take that!* Okay, time for a little honesty check. It's fun to play the victim, isn't it? There is a fair bit of power in being a martyr. You garner a certain amount of respect and attention that is reserved only for those who have suffered. And doggone it, why not? *I have suffered, why can't I enjoy a little bit of sympathy for what I've been through?*

Because it's not healthy, that's why. Martyr sympathy doesn't last very long. And a needy victim quickly grows tiresome. You know it's true. Bars, online chat rooms, and blogs are full of victims seeking an audience. Tough love time: no one wants to be in your audience. They want you to be well, to be healed, and to start living again.

Living again starts with forgiveness.

There, I said it. It's out there now. Are you still with me, or did you throw the book across the room? Life begins when you start to forgive.

Forgiveness is one of those misunderstood concepts that is actually very simple. We are called to forgive. Period. That's really all there is to it. Then why is it so stinkin' hard to do? Now don't confuse simplicity with ease. Forgiveness is a simple concept, but it takes great spiritual courage to achieve. Forgiveness is not easy. So strap on those brave boots, my friend, and let's start walking toward freedom, one step at a time.

"But you don't know how he treated me," you might say. "You don't know the lies he spread about me, and the way my reputation has been ruined." Or, "He took me for everything we had. He got the car, the house— everything. You don't know what it is like."

Let's look at someone else who was falsely accused, someone else who was judged wrongly and abandoned by those closest to Him. I'm talking about Jesus, of course. Jesus was accused of trying to usurp the government, He was accused of lying and being deceitful, and He was accused of blasphemy. The very people He came to save condemned Him to die. And not just a nice, humane lethal injection, but a brutal, excruciating, and humiliating crucifixion. The method reserved for the worst of criminals. An execution for the scum of the earth.

Before they actually nailed him up, the Romans whipped Jesus with a cat-of-nine tails. A type of whip that had several leather straps imbedded with shards of bone and metal, designed to rip out hunks of flesh with each lash. It was said that forty strokes would kill a man. Jesus received thirty-nine. They pulled chunks of His beard out of His face and beat Him with their fists and heavy rods. And then, in case He wasn't hurting enough, they put a robe on Him, and a crown of thorns was bashed onto His head. All of this was done publicly in the courts before He even began His climb toward the hill where He would die.

The Romans marched Him through the streets of Jerusalem in front of thousands, mocking and spitting on Him the whole time. I always wonder if there were people in that crowd who Jesus had miraculously fed just weeks before. Or, were there people who could see Him stagger up the hill only because He had healed their blindness, giving them sight for the first time in their lives? Were they mocking Him just to save their own skin? When they reached the execution spot, the

Romans laid Jesus down on the cross—on His back, which was so shredded that His ribs were showing. And then, they took massive spikes and nailed Him to the wood. They tacked a sign above His head making fun of Him, and then raised Him up—naked by the way—for all to see.

Crucifixion is not a quick death. You don't really die from the wounds at all. You suffocate to death. In utter agony, you try to pull yourself up by your nailed wrists and push yourself up by your nailed ankles so you can take a breath. Breath after breath. Up and down, pressing on spikes driven through the bones in your joints. For hours. Unfathomable pain. Breath after shallow breath. Until finally, you die.

This was the arena in which Christ uttered those famous words. High on a cross, displayed for all to see. This was the situation in which He cried out: *Father, forgive them, for they do not know what they are doing.* Luke 23:34

They knew what they were doing. They intentionally executed Him. But, they didn't really know. They didn't know that they were really executing the Son of God. They didn't understand that Jesus had come to save them. He knew the people were going to kill Him, and He came anyway. They didn't get that. From the very beginning, Jesus knew He was going to die. He knew how He would die. And from the beginning, Jesus knew He would forgive them.

Now, tell me again what it is your mate has done to you? How does that compare to what Christ went through?

There are probably little snatches here and there in our own stories that give us a glimpse of what Christ was feeling. Betrayal. Unfair judgment. Abandonment by those who were supposed to love us. But I bet for the vast majority of us, our experience pales in comparison to what Christ went through.

And yet, He chose to forgive. With one of His last, excruciatingly painful breaths, He chose to forgive. How can we do any less?

\*\*\*

If you're like me, after the initial shock of the whole crucifixion experience wears off, you might say something like: "But Jesus was God. He has supernatural ability to forgive. I'm just me—an angry, hurt, and very human woman who hasn't brushed her hair in three days. There is no way I can forgive." Hate to be the bearer of bad news, but that argument, one I tried myself, doesn't fly.

*Bear with each other and forgive whatever grievances you may have against one another. Forgive as the Lord forgave you. Colossians 3:13*

Boooo! Boo, ouch, and yuck! Forgive as the Lord forgave you. We just saw how Jesus forgave. Wholly, completely, and with His final, dying breaths, Jesus forgave. Forgive as the Lord forgave you. There's no caveat saying: "If you're the Son of God, or have God-like qualities, then forgive." Just a flat out, "forgive as the Lord forgave you."

Not only is it a command from God, it's a command with a consequence—or blessing, depending on how you look at it.

*For if you forgive men when they sin against you, your heavenly Father will also forgive you. But if you do not forgive men their sins, your Father will not forgive your sins.* Matthew 6:14-15

Now, this verse can bring about a whole lot of tricky theological debate. But, for our purposes, we're just going to take it at face value. After all, we're exhausted and angry, and verging on bitterness, right? I don't know about you, but I can only do so much deep thinking in that state. The Lord measures His forgiveness of you in the manner in which you forgive others. Your forgiveness of your mate has a direct impact on the way God forgives you.

A little word about sin. To us, there are big sins: murder, rape, being divorced by a lying cheating scumbag husband; and there are little sins: gossip, white lies, fudging the numbers on your taxes a bit. But to God, all sin is the same. Sin is sin. To a perfect God, whether you sin big or you sin small, it all looks the same. So, your sin, when you made up a rumor about your neighbor, my sin, when I said a bad word the other day, Judas' sin, when he betrayed Jesus, and your husband's sin, when he left you, *all look the same to God*. We are all sinners before God.

If God forgives me for my sins, and Jesus forgave Judas, the Romans, the Pharisees, Peter, and all the rest of them for what they did, then who am I to withhold forgiveness from my husband? When you withhold forgiveness, you are, in effect, saying you are better than God.

Father, forgive them, for they know not what they do.

Father, forgive me, for I'm a mess, and I need your help in forgiving my husband.

***

There's a common misconception about forgiveness out there. I often hear: "I can't forgive him. What he did was not okay. If I forgive him, then that's saying that everything he did to me doesn't matter." Forgiveness does not mean that what was done to you is okay. It is not okay when your husband "forgets" his wedding ring when he goes out with friends. It is not okay that he ran up a huge credit card debt in your name. It is not okay that he is turning the kids against you and refuses to pay child support.

Here is the strong truth about forgiveness: forgiveness does not mean that what has happened to you is okay. Because it is not okay. But other than the fact you have been wronged, forgiveness has nothing to do with what happened to you or who did it.

Forgiveness is not about them. Are you ready for this?

Forgiveness is about you.

Forgiveness is about finding freedom in letting go. I've heard it said that unforgiveness is like walking around drinking poison hoping the other person will die. A pretty powerful analogy. Are you drinking bitter poison hoping your mate will wither and die from it? Are you the lady in the grocery store line with the magazine? Ask yourself some hard questions. I'm not trying to embarrass you; I'm trying to get you to stop drinking poison.

Spewing hatred to anyone and everyone who will listen doesn't really hurt your mate; it hurts you. He doesn't care, and it makes you look like a fool. He's already moved on and is living life without you. It hurts, but it's true. Why are you still spending your precious energy and days living your life with him as your focus? You are not the focus of his life. Why is he the focus of yours? Does he deserve that? Of course not. Then stop giving him the honor of your time, thoughts, and energy! It is time for you to take back your life. It's time to move past the pain and start living again. It's time to forgive.

But how do I do that? Especially if my heart's not in it? It starts with a simple act of obedience. Being willing to think about forgiving is a start. Pray, asking God to give you the heart for forgiveness. Tell Him you want to follow His command, but you need help. Keep asking—daily, hourly if needed. I promise God will be faithful to help you forgive. He did it for me.

Next, I challenge you to forgive out loud. In privacy of course, but practice forgiveness by saying it out loud. "Phil, I forgive you for breaking your promises to me. I forgive you, Phil, for checking out when I was pregnant." Be specific about the actions you need to forgive, and put your spouse's name on them. Out loud. There is power in the spoken word. Jesus forgave out loud when He was dying on the cross. He could have thought it in His heart, especially since speaking was physically excruciating for Him. God would have known. But Jesus said it out loud. "Father, forgive them, for they do not know what they are doing." Say it out loud. Even if it's physically painful. Forgive your husband, out loud.

Secondly, you need to forgive yourself. *Oh no, you don't have to go there, do you?* Of course we do. This is about total healing, girlfriend. We're going to get into all those nooks and crannies and scrub away.

Sometimes we don't forgive ourselves because of the whole, "it's fun being a martyr thing." Remember, earlier in this chapter we talked about how no one wants to be in your martyr fan club? They don't. Get off the cross, honey—someone needs the wood!

Sometimes though, we truly do have a hard time forgiving ourselves. Most likely you're not completely innocent when it comes to your divorce. In my selfishness, I contributed to the breakdown of my marriage. What did you do that requires forgiveness? Maybe you need to forgive yourself for marrying a man you know you shouldn't have. Was your marriage an act of rebellion against your parents, social pressure or even God? Or was your husband not the only one who was lying in your relationship? Have your motives been questionable, if not downright deceitful? Were you a nag or a shrew, tearing down your husband in public just to humiliate him? Did you entertain thoughts of an affair or perhaps even act on those thoughts? Whatever your trespass, God has forgiven you. And if God has forgiven you, what right do you have to withhold forgiveness from yourself? Remember that whole thing about being better than God by withholding forgiveness from your husband? Same concept here. It's time to forgive yourself.

*For as high as the heavens are above the earth, so great is his love for those who fear him; as far as the east is from the west, so far has he removed our transgressions from us.*
Psalms 103:11-12

God's forgiveness is right there, waiting for you to accept it. He's already given it to you. Take it, and wrap yourself in His beautiful, sweet, tender forgiveness. Inhale and experience His gentle love for you. Breathe deeply in God's forgiveness of you. You are free, my friend. You are free from guilt and shame. God has removed your sin as far as the East is from the West. That's pretty far. In fact, East and West never meet. Don't be stubborn. Let God heal you. Forgive yourself.

\*\*\*

The thing about forgiveness is it's not just a one-time thing. The first time you forgive your mate is a really, really, big deal. But it probably won't be the last time you'll be given the chance to forgive. Do you like how I phrased that? *Given a chance to forgive?* It's all part of the growing process, getting to practice those tough tasks.

One-time forgiveness is not enough. If you have children together, you will most likely have more disagreements. Some are as minor as who pays for soccer league, and some will be major, possibly requiring intervention from the court. Or maybe your kids are grown and the issue is who gets the retirement investments, or you are bickering over who gets the lake house for the Fourth of July. Forgive, sister. Walk in freedom. Forgive.

And sometimes, it will not be the things in the now, but the issues in the past. Perhaps your ex-husband has passed away due to old age, or possibly an accident based on his bad choices. Or maybe, he's living somewhere off the coast of Sumatra with no electricity, and you haven't talked to him in several decades. Sometimes we have to forgive the memories. For those are the sinister ones. These memories are the ones that threaten your well-being, your peace. When they rise up late at night to mock you in your loneliness, forgive. When they taunt you as you watch other happy "complete" families at your child's graduation, forgive. When the memories of the past threaten to overtake your present, choose life, and forgive.

Peter—because he's awesome and says the things that we are all thinking and really want to know but don't have enough guts to ask—questions Jesus about how many times he should forgive someone who has wronged him. "Up to seven times?" Peter asks smugly. And Jesus tells him, "Seventy times seven."* Bam. Not just seven times, but seventy times seven. You get the point. There is no limit to how many times we are called to forgive someone. If this is discouraging for you, remember that there is no limit to how many times Jesus will forgive you. Focus on the One who taught us how to forgive, and not on the one who needs forgiving. "Father, forgive them, for they do not know what they are doing."

***

I hear people say all the time: "Well, I can forgive, but I can't forget." Let me challenge you by saying that this goes back to confusing what forgiveness is with feigning to be better than God. There are several meanings to the word "forget". Here, it is not talking about pretending like something didn't happen. If your husband was physically abusive, you need to forgive him, but you must also protect yourself and stay away from him. Your safety demands that you can't forget what happened.

What God is talking about is when you choose not to forget because you are harboring a grudge. You are nursing old wounds. Basically, when you choose to not forget, you are not really forgiving. The word "forget" is right above "forgive" in my Bible's concordance. The two words go hand in hand, and in fact, appear in several verses together. God is onto us. He knows how we like to make little loopholes. To not forget is to not forgive.

*For I will forgive their wickedness and will remember their sins no more.* Hebrews 8:12

The writer of Hebrews is actually quoting from Jeremiah. This whole forgive and forget concept made both the Old and New Testament—must have been important. Once again, if God is saying that He will not only forgive my sins, but won't remember them, then who am I to defy God by saying that I need to hang on to my grudges? Are the sins my mate committed against me greater than the ones I committed against Christ? All sin is the same in the eyes of God, and He forgives every last one of them. Then He remembers them no more. Learn from our Heavenly Father, sister, and remember no more the sins that have been done against you.

You thought going through a divorce is hard; forgiveness is even harder, but it is so worth it. God is waiting on the other side of forgiveness to open up His storehouses of blessings for you. Forgiveness will shed pounds off your life. Forgiveness gives you permission to put down the heavy burden of bitterness and start living again. People will see it in your face, and you will notice it in your spirit.

*Get rid of all bitterness, rage and anger, brawling and slander, along with every form of malice. Be kind and compassionate to one another, forgiving each other, just as in Christ God forgave you.* Ephesians 4:32

Put back the celebrity gossip magazine, leave that poor store clerk alone, and put down the poison you have been drinking. By choosing to forgive, you will be choosing life. Begin to practice forgiveness, one step at a time. Breathe life back into your weary soul. Choose life. Forgive and then forget.

*Matthew 18: 21-22

## Chapter 12

# COMPASSION AND MERCY

Compassion. I love that word. It conjures up images of a relief worker handing out food to starving children. Or the medical missionary doing surgery on a cleft palate, giving a young man the chance for a normal life. Compassion. It has the word passion in it, suggesting an action that is felt strongly but is done with tender care. Compassion is easy to have for those who are innocent and suffering. But compassion for my mate? He's certainly not innocent, and if he's suffering, well good, that makes two of us. Mercy for my husband? That's just not going to happen.

If you made it to this paragraph, that means your book has not been thrown across the room again. Or at least you went back and picked it up. So that's a good sign.

Lord, compassion and mercy are for refugees in Sudan. Not for ex-husbands. I opened up a vein working through forgiveness, and now you want me to extend compassion and mercy as well? Isn't forgiveness enough? I've got lots of compassion for tsunami victims and earthquake amputees—they deserve compassion. My spouse? He deserves to live in a yurt with a flatulent yak the rest of his life.

*Therefore, as God's chosen people, holy and dearly loved, clothe yourselves with compassion, kindness, humility, gentleness and patience.* Colossians 3:12

Ugh! God, I don't feel like "clothing" myself with any of those traits. I'm wearing my ticked-off outfit today. And it looks just fine, albeit a little uncomfortable. You're going to have to help me with this one.

Let's take a deeper look at this verse. It starts off addressing God's chosen people. It's not talking about the Jews here, so if you were thinking: "Whew, I'm a good, solid, full-blooded Gentile," you're not off the hook. Remember our chapter about the honor of being chosen? The one where God has called you to be a fine vase and not a chamber pot? This goes hand in hand with that. You have been chosen. "Therefore, as God's chosen people..." This verse is talking to you, china vase.

And hey! Look at that. What is the very first attribute on that clothing list? Compassion. Clothe yourself in compassion. Because God loves you, because He has chosen you, clothe yourself in compassion.

Notice it doesn't say: "Because there are sick Eskimos in Greenland" or "Because you are a glutton for punishment from a malicious spouse." The reason you should clothe yourself in compassion has absolutely nothing to do with the circumstances or with the recipient of your compassion. The one reason, the only reason, the non-negotiable reason to clothe yourself in compassion, is that you are loved by God, and you are chosen.

Compassion starts by understanding the suffering of others. Compassion starts with seeing people how God sees them. It's easy to understand that not having access to clean water can cause cholera. It's harder to see the internal emotional diseases of the people who hurt us.

Right now, I'm going to ask you to take a moment and pray that God will give you a compassionate heart for your husband. Ask God to give you the same heart for your mate that God has for him. The same heart God has for you. Ask God to let you see your spouse through His eyes. This is a hard request. It requires an unselfish heart and a forgiving spirit. But remember, we are taking a journey of healing and wholeness, and this is part of that journey. So, take a deep breath, and ask God to give you His perspective when it comes to your husband. What does God see that you may not?

An insightful friend once told me: "Hurting people

hurt people." There is profound wisdom in this simple little phrase. It is a law of nature. If your beloved family dog is injured, when you try to help him he will growl and maybe even bite you. A toddler, when denied their favorite toy, lashes out by hitting or biting. And our prisons are full of people who, unable to overcome their painful pasts, committed heinous acts. Hurt people hurt people.

Is it possible that your spouse is a hurt person?

Chances are, your husband is suffering and in pain. He may not act like it. He may not acknowledge it. And, here's a weird one, *he may not even know it.* But I'd be willing to bet that if your husband is hurting you by his behavior, he is hurting too.

The cause could be anything. Maybe his own father never told him he loved him. Maybe showing emotion was a weakness in his family, modeled by a cold mother. Maybe a teacher shamed him in front of his class, or maybe a respected coach told him he was worthless. Our lives are full of those poignant moments where someone or something inflicts great pain. By the time we get to adulthood, we are all carrying baggage. By God's grace, many of us are able to move beyond the pain and slowly drop our baggage piece by piece. But for many more, the bags get heavier, the lies believed become more sinister, and the hurt becomes all-consuming. Hurt people hurt people.

This was true in the collapse of my marriage, and I bet it's true for you as well.

Now, the temptation, for women especially, is to want to heal all that hurt and suffering. Perhaps that's why you married your spouse in the first place: to try to help him through it. Maybe you could show him the love he never had, be the cheerleader he always longed for. Sometimes that works. But unless your mate finds their true identity and worth in the Lord, you and your love will never be enough. You cannot heal the wounds of the past. You cannot fix your husband. God is not asking you to do that. Healing is God's job. Set yourself free from that burden.

But, God is asking you to see your husband with His eyes. Understand that your mate is acting out of some deep emotional and spiritual pain. Or perhaps He is believing the lies that come from those dark spiritual realms we discussed earlier. Jesus intentionally sought out those who were suffering. He placed His hands on the lepers who probably hadn't felt physical touch in years, He fed the people who were hungry, He healed people who were blind, and He cast out demons, giving people another chance at life. Jesus healed them because He had compassion for them. He understood their pain. You can't heal your husband's wounds, but you can understand that his actions are a result of them.

Do you realize the same compassion that Jesus

showed to the dregs of society, the same compassion that God extends to your husband, is the same compassion He is extending to you? Just as your husband is a wounded person, you are too. In God's eyes, your spouse is no different than you. But the good news is that God doesn't have a limit on His compassion.

*Yet the LORD longs to be gracious to you; he rises to show you compassion...* Isaiah 30:18a

The Lord longs to be gracious to you. He rises to show you compassion. Wow! There are no if/then statements here, no "If you make it to church three times a month, then God will show you compassion." No requirements or catches here, just a flat out truth. God longs to be gracious to you; He rises to show you compassion. God "gets up" to show you compassion. It's an action. It shows that He is being intentional. God is not ordering His angels to be the compassionate ones for Him while He does other things. God, Himself, gets up to show you compassion. And because God does it for you, He asks that you do it for others.

*As a father has compassion on his children, so the LORD has compassion on those who fear him.* Psalms 103:13

What a beautiful verse, once again showing the tenderness of our Heavenly Father. How privileged we are to be the children of God. I am so very grateful for my

Father who shows me compassion just as a good earthly father shows compassion to his own children. Did you know that your spouse is also God's child? It greatly pains the Father when His children hurt each other, but it doesn't stop His love for them. His compassion knows no bounds. No matter how deep your wounds are, no matter how much you have messed up and can't get it together, God will never run out of compassion for you. And because He has shown you such great compassion, God asks that you show the same compassion to your husband.

*** 

Mercy is a little bit different than compassion. Compassion is understanding someone's pain and taking pity on them on them in their difficult circumstances. Mercy implies that someone did something wrong, and they deserve punishment for it, but then choosing to withhold penalty. While compassion is an almost natural reaction to suffering, mercy is often the opposite of a natural reaction. Mercy implies that a wrong has been done, and retribution is deserved. Any wrongs been done to you lately? Got a desire to hand out some justice?

*Be merciful, just as your Father is merciful.* Luke 6:36

*Oh man! Now that's just not fair. Pulling God into the*

*whole thing. Of course our Father is merciful—He's God.* But Jesus wouldn't tell us in Luke to be merciful if it were impossible. He's telling us to be merciful because, even though it's not easy, it is possible.

I gotta say that when my husband lost his job while he was in the process of filing for our divorce, my first reaction was not particularly merciful. It was more along the lines of: "Serves you right for being such a jerk to everyone." Thankfully, I didn't say that out loud, and the Lord quickly gave me a heart of mercy for him. Losing his job was painful for Phil. He was angry about it for quite a while. Whatever the circumstances were, I knew that Phil was hurt by them, and I was sorry he was hurting. I even told him that. And by God's grace, I actually meant it.

Time and again, people came to Jesus and begged for mercy. The tax collector, the prostitute and the thief on the cross. Notice a common thread? These were some pretty big-time sinners asking Jesus for mercy. These were all people who deserved to be punished for their sins. But Jesus ate dinner with them, listened to their stories, and extended undeserved mercy. By Jewish law, He had every right to turn some of them in and even help with their stoning if He wanted. But instead, Jesus chose mercy. And He is asking you to do the same.

*The Lord is full of compassion and mercy.* James 5:11c

If God is full of compassion and mercy, how can we be anything less? Be merciful, because your Father is merciful. If God has shown mercy to you, then who are you to deny mercy to your spouse?

Mercy is hard. And it's a choice, a hard, painful, grumbling, begrudging, choice. If mercy does not come easy for you, ask God to give you a merciful heart. Ask Him to give you His eyes to see what is really going on. You already know your battle isn't really against your husband anyway, so seek the Father's perspective. Seek the heart of your Father. Mercy is much easier to extend when you are seeing your mate with God's insight. It's okay if your mercy meter doesn't go up overnight. It's a process that starts with being willing to be willing.

God is calling you to have compassion on your husband, and see his hurts with Jesus' eyes. He's calling you to show mercy to your mate, knowing he deserves punishment, but asking you to extend mercy instead. God is calling you to be a woman of compassion and mercy. As God's chosen one, you are destined for greater things. Learning to clothe yourself in compassion and mercy is part of your journey. For, in freely giving compassion and mercy, you will receive the same from your Father, and find great blessing in the letting go.

*Blessed are the merciful, for they will be shown mercy.*
Matthew 5:7

Hurt people hurt people. Starting today, learn to see your ex as God does. Be blessed. Clothe yourself in compassion, and choose to show mercy.

*Chapter 13*

# THE FIXER-UPPER

I spent the better part of a year trying to psychoanalyze my husband. I looked as deeply into his past as I could. I scrutinized his immediate family. I pulled out my old psychology textbooks and various diagnostic tools and tests. I talked with other women who had similar experiences. And, I received a lot of unsolicited advice. Many people had opinions on why Phil was doing what he was doing and when he would come back around. Some of their theories seemed plausible and some seemed far too simple, reducing my pain to sterile equations and patronizing conclusions.

I read divorce help books and books on the male psyche. I read stuff from learned Christian scholars and watched lots of episodes of Oprah. I read everything in the Bible about divorce and prayed night and day. I did all of this in an attempt to understand my husband, what he was thinking, and why he was doing what he was doing. I needed to know why my husband wanted out of our marriage, and what brought him to that point.

I tried really hard to make my marriage work. When I realized Phil was freaking out, I desperately grasped at things I could do that would make him want to stay. I did yard work, trimming the trees and shrubs. I attempted to cook him delicious meals—unsuccessfully. I tried to anticipate what would make him angry and then scurried around attempting to fix calamities that hadn't happened yet.

I remember the time our dishwasher wasn't working right. I wasn't sure what to do about it. I knew it was broken, but Phil had just criticized me for how much money we were spending getting ready for our baby. I didn't know if I should call a repairman which would cost money, or just let it go and do the dishes by hand until we had the money to get it fixed. Phil came home from work and blew up, blaming our defunct dishwasher on me. Why wasn't I getting it fixed? Why did he always have to be the one to fix the broken things? Why didn't I ever do anything around the house? During his rant, he pointed out a drawer in a cabinet that didn't open properly and accused me of being lazy and making him do everything. I was stunned. He knew I didn't know how to fix the drawer, much less the dishwasher. He, himself, didn't even know how to fix the dishwasher, so how would I? He stormed out of the house and left me in tears, blaming myself for not repairing things but not sure how to fix them anyway.

The next day, I called a repairman, dreading to see what the estimate would be. The kind man looked at our machine and said, "Lady, this area has rotted out, you just need a simple part, and it will work fine." And then he wrote down the name of the part and where I could get it cheap so my husband could fix our dishwasher.

So in my seven-months-pregnant-huge-waddling state, I drove twenty miles to the dishwasher parts store in a scary industrial area, bought the part, got directions, came home and installed that sucker myself. Seven months pregnant. Huge stomach and major back pain, bending over and reaching inside the dishwasher, trying to fix it, so my husband would love me.

During that year of deep thoughts, research, and exhausting myself trying to fix all that was broken, the fog began to lift. Somewhere along the way, I discovered another one of those life-altering truths. My divorce really wasn't about fixing my husband. It was about fixing me.

After reading all those books, I did gain some insight into his behavior. But all that gave me was knowledge. In my searching, I began to understand how his upbringing in the past was affecting our present. But understanding didn't fix my reality. I began to realize that I wasn't going to be able to fix him. I couldn't fix all the broken stuff in our house, I couldn't fix our marriage, and I couldn't fix the broken man I was married to.

The only thing I could control in my disintegrating marriage was myself.

So, instead of focusing all my energy on a man who I couldn't make happy, I decided to fix what I could: myself. I began to take a hard look at my flaws and the things I could control. I could control doing a better job at taking care of the house. I focused on tackling the messes immediately instead of letting them multiply, I focused on being a better cook, learning easy recipes and clever tricks from some dear women at my church, and I focused on getting ready for the birth of my child, taking nursing and labor classes.

There is great relief accepting that you can neither fix nor control your wayward spouse. In my effort to save my marriage, I had become a doormat, timidly walking on eggshells, hoping that my actions would make my husband love me. I eventually got to the point where I realized it didn't matter what I did, I couldn't save my marriage by myself.

And neither can you.

Your marriage is made of two people. You can only control one of those. Examine yourself to see what you can improve upon. Seek outside opinions on areas you can change for the better, and then let it go. Phil was hell-bent on leaving. Nothing I did was going to make a difference—to him at least. So I changed the target of my self-improvement projects. I worked on improving myself for me. And that was a whole lot more fun. I now know what a Dutch oven is (not a foreign appliance from the Netherlands at all) and how to use it. I make a mean loaf of homemade bread (with a bit of help from my bread maker). I bought a DIY from Home Depot and have repaired many an annoyance in my house. And every day after I get out of it, my bed looks like it came straight from a magazine. My bedroom can be a bit of a disaster, but my bed always looks nice, and that just makes me feel good. It's the little victories.

Take ownership of your life again. Take back what has always been yours to begin with. Take a hard look at your ugly spots. Do what you can to fix your flaws. Buy a bread machine and some pretty throw pillows, and set yourself free from having to fix what doesn't belong to you. You are an amazing woman who is on her way to healing, wholeness, and life. Don't give up!

My dishwasher still works by the way.

## Brass Tacks - Advice From the Sisterhood

Every divorce is different, as is every case, and every solution. I interviewed many women who went through divorces to get a wider view of what worked and what didn't. I asked them what they wished they'd known during the process and what they would have done differently. When appropriate, I will share a bit of their experiences and their advice. All names have been changed as well as identifying details.

## Chapter 14

# DO I REALLY NEED A LAWYER?

The legal process of a divorce can be intimidating in the best, and terrifying in the worst, cases. There are foreign legal words, mysterious processes, and people who all seem to want a piece of you—or at least whatever money you have left.

So do you really need a lawyer or can you just get a do-it-yourself kit? Every state is different, so it's crucial to know what your state requires for a divorce. Usually this can be found on a government website. Look for Divorce Proceedings or Documentations, etc. Some states require you to file for a divorce and then wait for six weeks, while others require some form of counseling before they will grant a divorce, particularly if there are children involved. And some states are quite lenient when it comes to filing for divorce, merely requiring a bit of paperwork and signatures. Usually, you will be required to produce the original marriage license or a certified copy and current identification, such as a driver's license or passport.

A do-it-yourself divorce is by far the cheapest option, but be careful not to mortgage your future just because you want to get the whole thing over with in an economical manner. Doing your own paperwork requires some level of trust in and from each person. You don't want to find out after the fact that he's been subsidizing his gambling addiction with your credit card or discover a hidden nest egg that should have been equally divided. But, if you think that both of you can be honest about your possessions and debt, and rationally divide up your property, a DIY divorce may be a good option. Just be very careful to read and re-read everything before you sign it.

The most common divorce proceedings include at least one lawyer. Unless you have very simple finances and property, my advice to you is to get a lawyer, even if you don't think there is that much to worry about. Even if you think he would never go there or try that, get a lawyer. This country is full of divorced women blindsided by ex-husbands who took advantage of their trust or naïveté. Don't be one of these women.

If you have minor children together, you must get a lawyer.

And don't just settle for any lawyer. Get a good

lawyer. Ask around. Get recommendations. A good lawyer can make all the difference in the world for you and for your children. A good lawyer will know all the tricks that people use to get out of this or that, hide things, etc. A good lawyer will close all the loopholes and protect you from all sides. For example: My divorce decree requires us to exchange tax statements every year. Since the child support for my daughter is based on his income, it's very important to know what he is making. My dear friend, Kayla, doesn't have such a clause in her decree. As a result, her ex-husband lies about what he makes and gives her a pittance in child support.

Another example is requiring both parties to split the cost of daycare or childcare. After a divorce, many women must go back to work, but the cost of childcare can be so expensive they can't make ends meet. My decree states that we split the cost of childcare, but my friend Sherry's decree does not. As a result, she is stuck paying all the costs for her three children while she tries to earn a living and support them all. Your ex may do the right thing when it comes to the finances, the cars, the house, or college tuition—but don't count on it. You must protect yourself and your future. Don't think of it as being antagonistic or aggressive. Think of it as being smart. If you don't have your best interests in mind, who will? Get a lawyer.

How do you pay for a lawyer if you don't have access

to the funds in the first place? Most judges will split the divorce costs between the two parties and take it out of the mutual bank accounts or property. Sometimes a judge may order one party to pay some or all of the costs. This can happen if one spouse is trumping up costs, being irrational, or dragging his feet in an effort to cost the other one more money. It doesn't always work that way, but again, a lawyer can advise you on that and plead your case in front of a judge. Most lawyers will meet with you to discuss your options, how to proceed, and how to pay for their services. This initial meeting is usually free of charge, and many are willing to work out a payment plan.

You don't have to be best friends with your lawyer, but it is important that you are comfortable with her. For instance, my lawyer understood that my number one goal was to try to save my marriage. I didn't want to get divorced, but I knew I had to take steps to protect myself. So we went into the whole process hoping that, at any point, I wouldn't need her anymore. Obviously, my marriage ended, and I did need her services, but I'm so thankful she respected my wishes and protected me in court.

Lawyers are also very good at taking the emotion out of the process as well as defining what's really important. There were many times when I was too emotionally wounded to fight or defend myself as needed, but I needed someone to make a rational decision or defend against an attack. My lawyer fought hard for me. I will be forever grateful to her.

Another option to consider is a mediator. Again, in each state, the qualifications and definitions differ, so do your research. In addition to each of our lawyers, Phil and I also used a mediator together. We had some very complicated financial issues to work out and many details concerning our young daughter. We realized that we could either decide our future, or leave it to a stranger in a black robe who didn't know either one of us or our child. Our mediator helped us decide multiple issues that otherwise would have been fought out in court—things we never would have thought of, but I am thankful she did. For example: putting in something about how I get my daughter for Mother's Day, and she is with her dad for Father's Day. Sounds simple, but my friend, Bethany, rarely gets to see her kids on Mother's Day because her ex "happens" to be vacationing in Europe with them. This also happens to her on her birthday and the children's birthdays as well. Not life-threatening, but certainly cruel, and easily accounted for in a solid divorce decree.

Phil and I interviewed three different mediators before we found one we both liked. She turned out to be a godsend, bringing up a wide variety of matters we needed to decide. For instance: My family lives across country, and I want to go home to be with them for Christmas. Usually, divorced parents alternate during their child's Christmas holiday—the first week with one parent, the second week with the other. But for us, cross-country travel dictated a need for a longer length of time. We decided that we would alternate Christmas and Thanksgiving every year giving Molly more time to spend with her grandparents instead of choppy and tiring travel during the holidays. Our mediator helped us put this and many other issues in writing, and then we signed a tentative agreement on them. Our agreements weren't technically legally binding until pronounced upon in the court, but they gave us the road map when our lawyers drew up our final decree. Although our mediator wasn't cheap, it was still less expensive than hashing out all those details in court. Lawyers cost more than mediators. Use a mediator when at all possible, and use a lawyer when it's not.

Divorces are hard, icky, and awful. But don't let the shock of being in one numb your common sense. Don't take anything for granted. Get a lawyer. We all know stories of someone who was taken to the cleaners by their ex. Don't be one of those stories that people tell in hushed tones while shaking their heads. Protect yourself and your future. Get a lawyer.

*Chapter 15*

# Putting Your Children First

Divorces are hard, but when children are involved, they can be devastating. While the adults each have some responsibility, the children are truly the innocent victims. We all know grown men and women who still suffer the scars from their parents' break-up. While you may not be able to save your marriage, you can do your very best to help your children cope with its demise.

There is an attitude that you must adopt to help you navigate almost any issue that arises where the children are concerned. The phrase is simple, but the instruction profound. **You must love your children more than you hate your spouse.** Basic in concept, but so very hard to do. Above all else, you must love your children more than the hurt, anger, bitterness, and sorrow—greater than the rage, betrayal, desire for revenge, and guilt. No matter what your spouse has done, is doing, or will do to you, you must love your children more than you hate him.

And this is why: no matter what your ex-husband has done, he is still their father. Children, especially young ones, have an innate connection to their parents. They just do. Even if their dad is in prison, they still love him and miss him. Even if mom skipped town and doesn't want to see her kids, they will still long for her. If you attack their dad, children take it personally and feel like you are attacking them. So every time you go on a rant—even if it's true—about how stupid, or hateful, or ignorant, or spiteful, or greedy their dad is, they will feel the need to defend him.

And when your children feel the need to defend their mom or dad, they are torn because they feel they are betraying you by wanting to defend their other parent. Talk about conflicted emotions. It's hard for adults to be torn between two warring factions they love, much less a child. Don't put your child in this situation.

My friend, Rachel, a well-adjusted forty-something adult, recently told me she hated both her parents for bashing each other in front of her and her brother during and after their divorce. *Hated.* Her dad really was a drunken womanizer, and her mom really was a belligerent, angry shrew, but it was still painful for her to endure the never-ending fighting between them. To this day, as a forty-something, even though she recognizes their unappealing natures, she visibly cringes at the memory of how her parents attacked each other.

Here is a truth: your children will eventually realize the true character of both their parents. Sometimes in high school, sometimes in college, and sometimes not until early adulthood. But, children do eventually understand that the rosy image of their parents isn't always true. This can be painful for a child. Remember when you discovered your dad couldn't throw a football or your mom couldn't cook a pork chop to save her life? Maybe the real truth is far more painful than this. But how much better for a child to gain this knowledge through her own maturity than from the rantings of an angry parent.

So, when you are tempted to get in a verbal fight with your ex, don't do it in front of the kids. When you can't stand the way he is behaving, don't bad-mouth him in front of your kids. When you want to call him every name in the book, don't. It may make you feel a little better for a brief moment, but it can scar your kids for life.

But what about the times when your ex's behavior hurts your kids? What do you say when dad doesn't show up for the birthday party, or when mom promises a shopping trip only to dump your child for a margarita night with the girls? You might be tempted to throw him under the bus, and rightly so. But take a deep breath, and acknowledge your child's feelings instead of bashing your ex. "I know you're really disappointed right now, Spencer. I will be sad with you. Why don't we go get an ice cream from Forty-seven Flavors instead?"

Then, if you need to, after your kids are in bed, call your best friend and vent to her.

Obviously, if the situation involves abuse or serious neglect, a child must be removed from that environment. Emotional or physical abuse is never ok, no matter whom the adult is. Don't be afraid to seek counseling for your children. A court may order it anyway, but it would be much better for them if you could find a nurturing counselor who can help them navigate their feelings and begin the healing process.

And finally, please know that your children are not doomed to a sub-standard existence because their parents are divorced. Your divorce will impact them, but it doesn't have to define them. This world is full of kids who have come through their parents' divorces and are ok.

Give your children this gift: protect them at all costs. Protect them from the hateful words, protect them from the real truth if necessary (at least while they are too young to handle it), and protect them from your own pain. Your children didn't ask for this. Their brains are not yet wired to handle all the grown-up emotions and feelings. Even if you can't save your marriage, you can do everything possible to help your children work through it.

*Chapter 16*

# MEMORIES AND OTHER IRRITATING LEFTOVERS

"I've got friends in low places where the whiskey drowns and the beer chases my blues away. And I'll be okay..." Admittedly an odd song to be *our* song, but it was. Good 'ole Garth. Phil and I used to country dance together, and Garth Brooks was hugely popular at the time. That song was played everywhere—two-steppin' joints, restaurants, and every radio station whether country or not from Texas to Toronto. I think we even played *Friends in Low Places* at our very conservative, no-alcohol-served, wedding reception. So many ironies...

And then Phil and I got divorced. But nobody bothered to tell Garth, or the radio stations, or the mass culture at large that felt the need to sing about their lowly social status in football stadiums at the top of their lungs. What was a fun, happy go-lucky song for the rest of America suddenly became a very painful kick in the gut for me.

Divorces are like that. All the inside jokes, the photo albums, the movie you saw on your first date, your favorite restaurant—all of these happy memories become reminders of something once so happy and hopeful, but now so painful.

In talking to several gals who survived their divorces, I discovered that we all handled the mementos of marriage differently. A lot depended on the memory associated with it. Or the memory that we wanted to remember. There is no one right answer about what to do with his mom's heirloom recipe for crème de la calorie (bake it proudly, and when asked, mumble something about an ancient family recipe lost long ago), but here are some ideas:

**The Wedding Gown**—So much time, energy, and emotion goes into a wedding gown. More than any other garment we wear. Our wedding dress carries our future dreams as well as our brilliant, gorgeous moment in the sun. That's a lot of pressure for a piece of fabric.

Married in 1994, my wedding dress was a glorious confection of beading, sequins, rhinestones, lace, and poof everywhere. Big poofy skirt, big poofy sleeves and a train that would've impressed Princess Diana. I think it weighed more than my dog. I *loved* my wedding gown. After the wedding, I had it dutifully preserved in a huge box that took tons of precious real estate in the crawl space under the stairs. I was under no illusion that my daughter might want to wear it one day. Thank goodness my own mom didn't have those dreams of me wearing her gown either. Her dress was one ugly concoction of daisies and yellowed polyester. But even though I knew my daughter would get her own dress one day, I still wanted to save my wedding dress just because I loved it.

After my divorce, my wedding gown no longer symbolized a beautiful future, it just took up a lot of space—and looked pretty outdated. Sniff! However, I thought it would make a fabulous costume. So I donated it to a theater company that puts on multiple shows all over our area. And, sure enough, I went to see *The Little Mermaid*, and guess who made an appearance in the final wedding scene? Yep, my old wedding gown was happily living a new life in the limelight that it was created for. With the stage lights and a cast of at least a thousand, my gown was truly dazzling, if I do say so myself. Ariel looked pretty good in it too. It made me so happy to hear the oohs and aahs of the little girls in the audience when she walked out encrusted in the best rhinestones the early 1990s could offer.

If seeing your gown under the stairs is too painful for you, get rid of it. Sell it or donate it. There are many charities that recycle and upcycle wedding gowns. You might make another bride's day by giving her the dress of her dreams. Or if your gown isn't quite the current style, as I said above, it might make a great costume for a local theater group or school production. If you want to sell it, ebay, Craigslist, and resale shops are great options. Don't expect to get all your money back though. Shoppers on these sites are looking for bargains. But, any money you make is more than you had before, right? Put it in your vacation fund.

And finally, it might make a great dress-up item if you have a little girl. If it's not too painful for you, your little one might love getting all gussied up in the dress her mama wore. I remember tromping around in my mom's wedding shoes —pink vinyl numbers with lots of rhinestones and a very sturdy heel. Pretty sexy, Mom.

**Your Wedding Ring(s)**—What do you do with your engagement ring? What about the band, the stones, his ring? Again, much depends on how you feel about them. Was the stone an heirloom from a relative on your side or his? Did you have the bands engraved? Did you spend months picking out matching sets, or were they quickies bought at the mall?

Unsure of what to do with my original ring, I still have it. I have thought about taking out the stone and re-mounting it in a necklace, or possibly saving it and giving it to my daughter as a graduation present in a different setting. When I got re-married, I took it into the jeweler to see if we could trade it towards our new rings, or get some cash for our honeymoon, but it wasn't worth all that much anymore.

My friend, Melanie, sold hers to help pay for bills, Diane still has hers in a safe deposit box, and Stacy wears her diamond in a necklace now. There is no wrong answer here. If you can't stand the sight of it, sell it and put the money towards a girlfriends' getaway or your child's college fund. If it still has sentimental value for you, hang on to it. There are no rules saying you have to decide right now. One day, when you are ready, you will know what to do with it.

**The Wedding Photos**—I think we've all heard stories about someone who, in a delicious state of revenge, burns her wedding pictures in a raging bonfire in the backyard. My friend, Ginger, did just that and hasn't looked back. If it is healing for you, burn them, bury them, or just throw them away. If you sob or feel rage rivaling the Incredible Hulk every time you pass your wedding album, it's okay to get rid of it. But it's also okay not to.

I kept my albums and photos, but not because I harbored some pathetic hope of the fairy tale having a miraculous happy ending. I kept them for a couple of reasons. First of all: I loved my wedding. I had the quintessential southern Dallas wedding. Big dress, big flowers, big bling. I loved the colors I picked. I loved the musicians we chose—a trumpet quintet, and I loved our reception location. My sweet parents spent a ton of money, and I loved everything about my wedding. The groom—well, obviously that part didn't turn out so well. But, I have been able to separate the happy memories of that time of my life from the painful ones later. For, it was indeed, a joyful day. All the people I loved the most were there, and I felt beautiful. I choose to remember it that way.

Secondly, I kept the pictures for my daughter. She loves to look through them and marvel at how handsome her father looked and how sparkly everything was — Texas bling at its best! Even though she wasn't there yet, it is still part of her history. If you have children, consider them in your decision whether or not to keep the photos. You can always box them up now and bring them out when the memories are less painful. Or, if your children are adults, ask them if they would like some of them.

Your photos of your wedding and your life with your ex document your history. Even though the ending of that chapter of your life is painful, it is still part of your journey. Hopefully there were some happy times here and there. Choose to remember those as you begin the next chapters in your life.

**Your Mutual Friends**—Yikes! What do you do when all your friends are couples and you're now a single? What do you do when you have the same friends as your ex? Divorce is hard on everyone, even your friends. They feel forced to pick sides and can feel uncomfortable inviting one of you, but not the other, to events and gatherings.

Know that this phase can be a little awkward for a bit, but it doesn't last that long. The very nature of divorce will force your friends to pick a side, for lack of a better phrase. They can't invite you both over, so they will either pick one of you, or sometimes neither of you. They will either feel comfortable  inviting you to their barbecue, or they won't. A lot of how they respond will be in reaction to how you're handling things.

Phil and I had attended the same couples Sunday school class for years, and most of our friends were in that class. We all got married at the same time, and we had kids around the same time. We were all in a similar life phase. And then, Phil and I got divorced. Suddenly, I was the only one in my group of friends who wasn't married. To their credit, they kept inviting me to join them in their lives. And I kept going. For years after my divorce, I kept going to our "couples" class which eventually became just an "adults" class to be more inclusive. And after a while, I wasn't the only single one there anymore. They invited me on campouts and game nights, and I went. Sometimes, it was hard being the only one without a spouse. But it was harder sitting at home by myself. I joined other groups too and took up new activities where nobody knew I had even been through a divorce. God gave me new friends.

Your friend situation will change a little bit. It just will. But your true friends will still remain loyal. And the Lord may surprise you with new friends who will enrich your life immensely.

**Your Name**—Do you keep his last name, or do you go back to your maiden name? Again, there is no wrong or right answer here. Samantha kept her married name because her maiden name was really hard to pronounce and she never really liked it anyway. Angela kept her married name so she and her children would share the same last name. And Heather kept hers just because she didn't want to mess with all the paperwork to change back her driver's license, bank accounts, billing statements, and credit cards.

I decided to go back to my maiden name. My married name was more unusual, and honestly I didn't want my identity to be associated with my ex-husband anymore. I didn't want to carry his name on everything I ever did for the rest of my life. It's true, my daughter and I have different last names, which makes it harder at the airport and for her teachers at times. But I figured she will probably change her name one day when she gets married anyway, and the TSA guards are always very understanding. She's not the first kid with a different last name than her mom.

And I would present to you one more option: Johanna took an entirely new last name. She didn't want to keep her husband's last name, but she also didn't want to go back to her maiden name. Her parents were abusive and that name only brought back painful memories. So, she renamed herself. She picked a last name she liked, put it in her divorce decree, and that's who she is now.

There are no rules when it comes to changing your name or not. Just be sure that you put it in your divorce decree. Otherwise you have to go back to court and do it separately. And after going through a divorce, who wants to spend any more time in court?

**Your Anniversary, Your Divorce Date, Valentine's Day**—It's part of human nature to commemorate significant days in our lives, which is fun when you get to spend a weekend away or enjoy a special restaurant. But then suddenly, August 16th isn't so much fun anymore. And it doesn't go away. August 16th comes around pretty much every year.

The hardest day for me was Valentine's Day. All those sappy commercials with good-looking guys buying diamonds, flowers, and chocolates. I don't even like chocolate, but there were years I would've eaten the cardboard heart-shaped box if it had come from someone who cared about me.

After being an emotional basket case watching

*Laverne & Shirley* re-runs that first lonely Valentine's Day, I decided things would have to change. The next year, I made an appointment at a sheeshy salon, got my hair and nails done, and got a massage. Just because a man wasn't there to treat me well didn't mean that I had to sit at home and mope. So I didn't. Soon I looked forward to Valentine's Day. It became the one day of the year when I allowed me to spoil myself.

Do yourself a favor and plan something fun on those hard days. Whether it's your anniversary or a holiday that's difficult, be kind to yourself. Treat yourself to a spa day, a shopping spree, or go do an activity you've always wanted to try—bungee jumping anyone? Banish the negativity that comes from sitting around feeling sorry for yourself and go create new memories for that date. Make Laverne and Shirley proud.

**Our Song/Movie/Restaurant, etc.**—As a general consensus among the gals I talked to, it seems the sentimental association with these fades with time. Eventually, you'll go to that restaurant with friends again, you'll hear that song on the radio, and you'll see that movie again without immediately bursting into tears. Just give it time.

In the beginning, there are so many reminders and triggers. They seem like they're around every corner waiting to ambush you and send you into a puddle of tears in front of bewildered strangers. It's possible I cried

129

in public when *Friends in Low Places* came on in the elevator. Nothing like a stranger in a business suit fishing around for a hankie and awkwardly patting you on the shoulder while you both think the 54th floor can't come soon enough. But these things are just that: things. They only have the power you give them. If something happy happened at Burger King, acknowledge it, order your onion rings, and then move on. If that perfume was his favorite, wear it on a date if you still like it, or give it to Goodwill if it reminds you of his grandma. It's okay. The memory police aren't hovering over your shoulder waiting to smack you if you let go of something.

Likewise, feel free to take back the things or experiences you want to keep. My ex-husband and I were on the same cheerleading squad together in college. I loved being a cheerleader. And even though he was part of much of my collegiate cheering experience, I don't let that ruin my experience of it. I enjoy attending football and basketball games as an alum, and I have since taught several cheerleading classes in partner stunts and gymnastics. Reclaim those parts of your life that are important to you. Just because he walked out the door doesn't mean you have to throw out the box of pompons after him.

Memories are just that: memories. Some will be happy, some won't. They are a part of your history, but they don't have to be part of your future. File away the ones you want to keep, acknowledge the ones you don't, and take a deep breath and turn on the radio. Garth Brooks and all his friends are waiting to raise a glass with you.

*Chapter 17*

# Taking the High Road

Take the high road. Turn the other cheek. Let go and let God. Stand firm. "Vengeance is mine," says the Lord. Nothing brings out the trite sayings and scripture quotes like a good tragedy in your life. And while most of the sayings, and of course all the scriptures, are valid, it can make for a very confusing spiritual journey. Do you have to be a doormat to honor God?

Jesus was the ultimate example for us, modeling meekness and submission—to the point of death! But then, the Bible is also full of stories in which God or His people fought, and fought hard, without any intention of submitting, much less dying. The Israelites did very little cheek-turning when they were taking over the Promised Land. So how do you know when to fight like an Israelite or when to imitate Jesus?

It starts with a key character trait: integrity. Integrity and a whole lotta prayer. Walk daily with the Lord and battle with integrity. Easy, right? Hah!

One day, your ex will have to account for everything he's done. He will have to answer for his selfish actions, his hateful words, and his deceitful deeds.

And so will you.

Hopefully you've figured out by now that you can't control what your spouse does. Life would have been so much smoother if you could. But even though you can't control him, you can control what you do. This is one of those precipitous times in life when you make choices that can haunt you for the rest of your life. Don't be one of those people who look back on their behavior and say, "I'm not proud of this, but I keyed his truck, or shaved his cat, or spread liquid death all over the lawn in the middle of the night..." In a fit of rage, my good friend, Victoria, drove her husband's car into his office building. True story. She's not proud of that – well actually, she still kinda is. But she admits it wasn't the smartest thing to do.

Keeping integrity in mind, know that there are some very big things that you should fight for, but there are also things that you should probably just let go. If he has his rotating girlfriend du jour over when your kids spend the night with him, you might want to fight that. Put it in the divorce decree that when the kids stay with him, the girlfriend does not. If he really wants to fight you for the electric cheese grater (even though it was your idea to register for it for your wedding), it's ok to let that go.

I know you know this deep down in your heart, but I'm going to remind you. Stuff is just stuff. It really is. Your stuff doesn't define you, it doesn't love you, and it can't save you. It's not worth killing yourself to hang on to every last tea cup or potted plant you can. God is quite capable of giving you more stuff, or even better stuff if He wants to. But it's still just stuff. And you'll probably have to dust it, organize it, and repair it so one day you can sell it at a garage sale anyway.

Be careful not to expend too much energy and finances fighting for the mutual stuff. Trust me, you'll need that energy and those finances later. Do your best to divide the stuff equitably and without malice. It's so easy to fight for the cheese grater, not because you like cheese droppings, but just because you know he wants it—just to make his life miserable. But realize that it works both ways. He may go after the self-retracting purple garden hose just to tick you off. Again, you can't control him, but you can take away his power by just letting him have the dumb garden hose. Don't become one of those sad stories we all hear about—five years of litigation over the wheelbarrow, resulting in bankruptcy of both parties, and then the children end up as tween felons because the fighting scarred them for life. Break that vicious cycle of retribution. Take the high road and just don't play the game.

Integrity applies to your words as well. We've

already talked about not bashing your ex in front of your kids, but it goes beyond that. I know you want to plaster it all over the internet what a scumbag he is. I can admit to a bit of admiration for those women who put up billboards on the highway telling the world their husband is a cheater. But the truth of the matter is that, other than for a moment of titillating scandal, no one really cares. They're only interested for entertainment. By broadcasting your pain and telling everyone in town what a jerk your ex is, you are becoming fodder for the gossip mongers. When it comes down to it, isn't your divorce humiliating enough without helping people laugh at your situation?

Your real friends will truly care. But they're probably not the audience of your internet smear campaign. Walk in integrity. Don't slander. Don't gossip. Hold your tongue. Walk in meekness, not bitterness. It just mires you in the muck longer than necessary and doesn't honor the woman God is trying to help you be. And besides, you want people to be glad to see you coming, not run the other way, right?

***

But what about the times when you must stand your ground and fight? It was Jesus who instructed us to turn the other cheek, so how do you know when, or even if, it's ok to take off the gloves and put up your dukes?

Jesus operated in meekness because He had a very specific task to do. Jesus' entire goal, His entire purpose for coming to earth was to take our place in death, rise from the dead, and give us the gift of being with Him in heaven one day. This is not your life's purpose. Can I get a Praise God?!

Your goal is to walk in integrity and meekness, but then to fight hard when you need to. Not fight dirty, not fight in revenge, but fight for the important things. Child support: worth fighting for. Fair division of property and debts: most likely worth fighting for. Protecting your kids from abusive behavior: fight tooth and nail. Pray earnestly for the Lord's protection, for His wisdom, and for Him to go before you in battle. Then strap on your helmet and see what God can do.

Act in integrity both in court and the court of public opinion, and let God handle the rest.

Just a word about revenge. Oh what a delicious word—even saying it in my head makes me want to smile my best evil smile and give a good cackle. Everyone loves a juicy revenge story. And women, especially, are all about the retribution. Hell hath no fury like a woman scorned, right?

Even God supports revenge. With one small caveat: He wants to do it Himself. God doesn't want you taking revenge on your ex because He wants to do it for you, on your behalf. Kinda cool, huh?

Do not take revenge, my friends, but leave room for God's wrath, for it is written: *'It is mine to avenge; I will repay,' says the Lord.* Romans 12:19 with reference to Deuteronomy 32:35

In my darker moments, I have to admit there was something so appealing about the phrase, "God's wrath." Don't deny God the ability to avenge you by doing it yourself. Whether it is in this life or the next, whether or not it's your idea of what fair vengeance should be, I'm guessing God will do a far better job at it than you posting your pathetic story on a billboard. So let it go. Don't give any more of your precious self over to your ex by plotting his humiliation and ruin. Lay it at God's feet, and let Him be the defender of your name.

It has been said that the best revenge is living well. Do yourself a favor and let go of the need for revenge. Live your life well, and some day, you just might get the last laugh.

*Chapter 18*

# IF I SIGN THE PAPERS, AM I GUILTY?

Irreconcilable Differences. Even now that phrase turns my stomach. That was the box I had to check when I signed my divorce papers. But I felt like I was lying. Phil and I had some major marriage issues—but they weren't irreconcilable. I was willing to forgive him, willing to work on my flaws, and willing to do whatever it took to heal our marriage. So how could I, in good conscience, sign my name to a lie?

How hard are you supposed to fight for your marriage? After all, you took a vow to be faithful and honor your commitment to your husband. A vow for life. If you sign the papers, does that mean that you have broken your vow? If you agree to the divorce, does that mean that you will always be branded a sinner, never again to feel God's blessing on your life?

In talking with others who have gone through a

divorce, this was one of the most painful regrets that many had. I could've fought harder to save my marriage. I should have refused to sign the papers. Agreeing to the divorce makes me just as guilty.

First of all, even if you get divorced, God can still save your marriage. An official divorce doesn't mean that it's over forever. We've all heard stories of divorced couples reuniting, sometimes decades after their divorce. A divorce decree doesn't scare God. He is a master at restoring broken lives and broken marriages. It's not common, but this happy ending may be yours one day.

Or it may not. When Phil was behaving really badly, I was horrified to realize that I might have to divorce him. He had completely checked out of our marriage, was lying to me about his whereabouts, and wouldn't talk to me. Literally. He would come home from work, go to the other bedroom he had moved into, and go to bed. At 5:15 pm. For weeks.

I finally moved in with my family in an effort to get myself and my daughter out of a caustic situation. I hoped, perhaps naïvely, that Phil would recognize the gravity of the situation and would agree to counseling. He didn't. He was furious at me and said whatever shred of reconciliation that might have been was now gone. But yet, he didn't do anything. For over a year, we lived in this limbo hell. He didn't love me, didn't want to be married to me, but wouldn't divorce me either.

In tears at a Bible study, I asked for prayer (for the thousandth time.) *Am I going to have to divorce my husband?* I didn't believe in divorce. I had fought so hard for my marriage. I had remained faithful to my husband and my marriage in the darkest times. But what I had wasn't a marriage at all. It was an insult to what God had designed marriage to be, and it certainly wasn't what I wanted my daughter to model her marriage after one day. *Was I going to have to divorce him?*

The wise leader of the Bible study took me aside and gave me a lesson about God and His laws. He told me the biblical story of how before he became king, David was running for his life. Even though David had already been declared as God's chosen for Israel, Saul, the current king, was trying to kill him. David and his men were hiding in the hills, fleeing from cave to cave and other areas across the countryside. And they were starving. The Bible tells how, in desperation, David entered the temple at Nob.* With the priest's permission, David took five of the twelve loaves of the offering that were sitting on the altar. This was an offering that the people had given. It was intended first for the Lord, and then the priests. The priests were allowed to eat it after one week, since their "job" was in the temple instead of out in the fields. Messing with the showbread was a high crime, punishable by death. But David was not punished. Why?

Because, the Bible study leader explained, God has laws, and then He has higher laws. And the higher law here was the Law of Mercy. David and his men were fugitives, and they were hungry. The temple had food. David and his men needed to eat. So they ate the "forbidden" holy food, and it was okay. The higher law of mercy prevailed over the sacrificial law of the food offerings. David wasn't punished, and in fact, went on to do some pretty good things for the nation of Israel.

So, when I was faced with the awful possibility of having to divorce my husband, the Lord stepped in and offered me His higher law of mercy. Phil had already physically and emotionally left our marriage. He ceased being my husband long before he moved out. He had been unfaithful in so many ways. He didn't love me, and he didn't want to be married to me. So even though I might have had to send him the papers, it was really he who did the divorcing.

As it turned out, Phil did finally file for the divorce. But only after the Lord had granted me peace about the situation. I had fought and fought, and I knew that one day, if my daughter asked me if I had done everything I could, I could answer yes. And most importantly, I know that I can stand before the Lord and say I did everything I could to honor my marriage. I clung to this truth when I signed my name and checked the box for Irreconcilable Differences.

If you feel guilt about your marriage dissolving, it's time to let that go. You are only one half of your marriage. Even if you were the one who had to file, I'm guessing it's because the situation had become so unbearable, you didn't see any other way. Walk in the higher law of mercy, sweet sister. The Lord is not holding it against you, so how do you justify wallowing in your regret? You can't. Let that burden go. Kick that guilt to the curb, and walk in freedom!

But what if you took an easier road? (If there is such a thing.) What if you know you could've done more, that you didn't fight as hard as you promised you would? The good news is that God is not stingy with His forgiveness. Jesus paid a high price for it—He's not about to withhold it. Even if you didn't honor your marriage vows or know you could have done more, there is mercy and grace for you too. You cannot change the past. You can't change who you married, and you can't change your past failures. God promises forgiveness to all who seek it. In fact, He forgave you long before you ever knew you needed it.

Shame and guilt are not part of God's plan for you. Remember? God has plans to prosper you, not to harm you. God wants to give you life and life more abundantly, not imprison you in a lifetime of regret. God forgives our sins and never re-visits them again. Ever.

*For I will forgive their wickedness and will remember*

*their sins no more.* Jeremiah 31:34

So, if God has forgiven you for whatever part you own in the failure of your marriage (even if it's all of it), what right do you have to carry around that guilt? None! I've heard too many stories of women who can't let go of the past. Melissa re-married after her divorce. Her current husband is a wonderful, godly man who passionately loves her and their three children. But, she still has nagging regrets about signing the papers for her previous divorce. She has resigned herself to a lifetime of self-inflicted shame for agreeing to a divorce she didn't want.

Ladies, hear me well. God is not holding your mistakes against you. He's not. Your next marriage is not doomed to failure because you signed the papers, or hired an attorney, or bickered in court, or fought in front of your kids. God remembers your sins no more. It's time for you to do the same. Do everything you can to save your marriage, and then let it go. You can't force him to stay. You can't force him to see a counselor, work on the issues, or want to be married. Be faithful to your spouse and your marriage. But when it's over, let it go. Throw off that smothering blanket of guilt that Satan keeps handing you. Live the life God intended for you—a life clothed in forgiveness, freedom, and blessing.

*1 Samuel 21:1-9

## Chapter 19

# DATING, AGAIN

"What man will ever be interested in me?" I asked through tears to a good friend at her kitchen table. I had a toddler, no strong income source, and would soon be a divorced woman. Not to mention all that fun emotional divorce baggage that was now mine. There's a man magnet if I've ever seen one. And I wasn't even sure I wanted to start dating again anyway. Didn't I already serve my time in that mad hunt for a mate? See how well that turned out? The thought of starting over was overwhelming.

"A good man. A godly man. That's the kind of man who will want you," my friend reassured me. Although I had my doubts, I was grateful for her encouragement. I didn't necessarily want him at that moment, but I had to admit, the idea of a good, godly man sounded really appealing.

Dating—again. Another one of those swell activities you get to revisit as a result of being divorced. Actually for me, it did end up being a lot of fun. But mainly because of God's grace and following some wise guidelines which are highlighted below.

I remember being shocked when I realized that I was attracted to a man who wasn't my husband. It was a brief encounter—one of those moments where you exchange friendly banter and a smile, and then realize afterwards that he was kinda cute. I had only had eyes for Phil for so long, it rattled me a little. For well over a decade, I hadn't allowed myself (rightly so) to look at another man, much less consider if he was attractive. It was more than a little weird. But looking back, I know that was the Lord gradually bringing me to a place where I would be ready to date again.

## Until it's Final, the Market is Closed

Let me be clear. Until you are divorced, you are married. Sounds a little obvious, right? But I have met so many women who seemed to be a little fuzzy on the boundaries while they were going through their divorce. So, while you are separated, you are married. While your divorce is stuck in litigation, you are married. Even if he is living with someone else, has completely abandoned you, and has moved on with his life—until your divorce is final, you are still married. This means you are not free to date, to peruse websites, or to tell interested prospects that you are available. Until you are single, you are married.

I know, I've heard all the arguments. By that point it's just a piece of paper. My husband checked out long ago. Don't I have the right to have a little fun? I met a great guy, but he may move on if I don't show interest.

I was in church with my mom and grandmother who were visiting from Texas. My mom is a mighty prayer warrior, and I had been praying that the Lord would show us someone who could use prayer or an encouraging word from the Lord. My mom has a gift for that sort of thing. After the service was over, this cute guy walked up to us and asked if we wanted to go to lunch with him. No lie. This good-looking guy, I'll call him Troy, was new to our church and was wanting to get to know people. I know I had been asking God for someone who needed encouragement or prayer, but a handsome single guy my age was not what I was envisioning!

So, along with my two-year-old daughter, we all went for Mexican food after church. Molly was potty training at the time, and I remember looking down in horror as she jumped out of her high chair and headed towards the bathroom. Her very full diaper was barely clinging to her ankle as she galloped down the aisle. I don't remember if this was before or after I had mentioned to Troy that I was in the process of getting divorced. Lovely. Can you imagine a more romantic introduction? I sure can't. Potty training blowout, and my divorce being finalized that week, so hey baby, ya wanna go out? God really has a sense of humor.

Against all odds, Troy did ask me out. How fun to be asked out on a date again! But, my heart sank as I had to tell him no. Because, even though it was almost over, technically my divorce wasn't final yet. I was still married. Remember when my friend had encouraged me about a good godly man in the future? Well, she was right. Troy was a good and godly man; he said no problem. In fact, he was divorced himself and was completely empathetic to what I was going through. He also understood that I wanted to honor my marriage and my vows to the end. He respected my wishes. A good and godly man who was not scared of a potty-training toddler and was willing to wait until my divorce was final. How cool is God?

After my divorce was official, Troy and I started to date, and I began to come back to life again. Troy laughed at my jokes and thought I was pretty. It had been so long since I felt pretty. When he put his arm around me the first time, I nearly jumped out of my skin. Goose bumps and hot tingling feelings—junior high anyone? It was exciting.

But, it was also a time when I needed to be extremely careful. And you do too.

## Be Careful Not to Jump Back in Too Soon

When you begin to date again after your divorce, you experience a boatload of crazy emotions. Most of them are good, but only if you keep them under control with a healthy perspective. Many dormant, and even forgotten, needs and desires are re-awakened when you start going out again. The need to be liked and loved. The need to be held and touched. The need to be understood and appreciated. The need for a companion in life.

Hear me now, sister. No man will ever be able to make you complete, heal your heart, or be all that you need. Men are fun, and it sure is nice to have someone to enjoy life with. But a man cannot put the broken pieces back together. Don't ask him to do that in your life. It's simply not fair and will set you up for more heartache.

The general thought is that you wait a year for every five years you were married before you start to date again. I didn't technically follow this rule to the letter, but my divorce also took three years to process, so I had plenty of waiting time.

Do not date too soon after your marriage. Both Laura and Hillary made this mistake. Laura was so lonely she latched on to the first guy who showed an interest in her. He was emotionally abusive, and her self-esteem, already fragile from her divorce, completely shattered. It took her several years to heal from both destructive relationships.

Hillary fell hard for a guy who was just using her. She knew what he was up to but was enjoying his attention so much that she didn't care. Both these women are intelligent and gorgeous. But they were so wounded from their divorce, they were unable to make good decisions in their relationships. They both said they wished they had waited longer before they started dating again.

If you are not emotionally ready to date, don't. It will only end up causing you further pain down the road. If you think you're ready, and you get in an unhealthy relationship, stop. Just stop. Both Laura and Hillary are real women with real stories and real warnings. Remember those wise principles about successful dating I mentioned earlier? This is one of them. Do not date too soon after your divorce. Wait until you and your heart are ready.

## Be Careful What You Fish For

So once you decide you're emotionally healthy enough to date, how do you do it? After my divorce, I realized there were two single guys at my church who weren't old enough to be my father. Troy and I dated for a while, but even though he was a fantastic guy, I eventually realized he wasn't the right guy. We amiably parted ways, and he has since married a wonderful girl who is just perfect for him. I was able to attend their wedding and was so very happy for them both

After having exhausted the two choices at my church, I began to look around to see who else might be a worthy prospect. Hmmm. Once you're out of college, the dating options dwindle dramatically. There was my church, the theater groups I was involved in, and the bar scene. My theater friends were either gay or had way too much angst to be considered. And the bar scene... well, yuck. I'm not a big drinker, at all—the bar scene never appealed to me before I got married the first time. Fifteen years later, it was still pretty icky.

Girls, here's another important tip. You catch what you fish for. And it matters what pond you're fishing in. In general, there were no husband-worthy guys at my local bar. Husband-worthy guys are not hanging out at bars doing lurid bar things trying to impress bar-type girls. A short skirt and multiple drinks will get you attention, but what kind of guy are you attracting? Ladies, what pond are you fishing in, and what bait are you using? You catch what you fish for.

I wanted one of those good, godly men. They were out there—not in droves, but they were there. Above all else, I wanted a man who loved the Lord more than I did. Being a little older and wiser the second time around, I cared a lot less about physical appearance and wallet size and a lot more about where a man was in his walk with God. I knew if he passionately loved the Lord, he would love me. I knew if he put God above all else, then no matter what, we would be okay.

I decided to try online dating. First I gave eHarmony® a try and eventually ChristianMingle®. I had good results with both of those sites. Here's why: I was really picky about the crucial things, and flexible about the rest of it. When you fill out your online profile (there are several great dating sites out there), you can be as specific as you want. I had a couple of non-negotiables. He had to be a Christian who actively went to church. ChristianMingle lets you pick specific denominations if you want. There is a big difference between, say, a Catholic and a Pentecostal. And I wanted a man who regularly went to church. While this doesn't guarantee godliness, I figured it upped my odds versus a guy who went only on Christmas and Easter just to keep his mom happy.

Another non-negotiable for me was a non-smoker and minimal drinker. Not making an indictment about either of these things. They were just important to me. A good site will let you be specific about your non-negotiables.

And then after that, I got pretty flexible. I had preferences and knew what I liked, but I also knew that God knew what I needed. I didn't want to limit God by telling him the exact kind of man I wanted. So I put in parameters, but there was wiggle room. When you are deciding what kind of man to fish for, make sure that you are open to what kind of man God wants you to catch as well. After all, doesn't He know what is best for you?

A word about paying for a site membership or just using a freebie. In general, the man who is willing to pay for a site is going to be a higher quality person and be more intentional about his search for the right woman. He will probably feel the same about you. Don't troll with the bottom feeders. Be willing to put the effort in a higher quality site and the catch will be higher quality as well.

Another dating tactic is to simply spread the word that you are on the market. Let your friends and family know you are ready to date again. These are the people who know and love you most. These are the people you want playing matchmaker for you. When they ask if you want to be set up, say yes! What's the worst that can happen? A couple of hours spent with a guy who waxes his nose hairs (or clearly doesn't but really should) will give you great comedy material for dinner with the girls later on.

## Be Smart, Be Safe

A quick word about safety here. Any date you go on needs to be in a public place. Period. If things go well, there's plenty of time for a cozy in-home movie night later. But in the beginning, always, ALWAYS, meet in a public place first. Don't be stupid. No matter how nice a guy sounds, no matter how cute his pic is, and no matter how much he asks, do not meet him at his house, or yours, for the first couple of times. If he insists on this, run the other way. I actually joined my friend Rebecca on her first date with a guy she had never met. We were both freshly divorced, and she just didn't feel good about meeting him alone. I did bring a book and planned on getting a separate table if things went well for the two of them. Nothing like being a third wheel at a table set for two. But the guy was a little odd and after some group chitchat, drinks and nachos, we said thanks but no thanks. Trust your instincts. If something feels off, it probably is.

## Get in the Boat!

And now for you wallflowers—you didn't think I'd forget about you, did you? Maybe you'd like a date, but you're just kind of hoping it will somehow magically happen. *If it's God's will, He will cause Brad Pitt (who is suddenly professing a deep faith in the Lord) to walk in here, find me irresistible, and sweep me off my house-shoed feet to live happily ever after in our bungalow for two with my cat.* Here's the deal. If you're not fishing, you're not going to catch anything. The tuna is not going to just jump in your boat. God can and will bring the right guy your way—in His perfect timing—but you've got to do your part. Get your hair cut and styled, buy an outfit you feel pretty in, fill out that online profile, join a social group, and get out there. Last time I checked, nobody ever caught a fish by sitting on the shore dreaming about a fried fillet.

One final note. If dating again scares you to death, it's okay. It can be intimidating, especially if you've been married for a long time. It is hard to pretend to be attractive when someone has told you for years how ugly you are. It is not easy to put yourself out there when someone has broken your trust and crushed your spirit. If you're truly not ready, that's okay. But be sure you're not just making excuses either. There may be a sweet man—a godly man—out there who has been waiting for you. He just hasn't met you yet. Help him out. Put on some lipstick and some scandalous shoes, and go on a date. Happily ever after may be your ending after all.

## Dating Tip Recap

1.  It's Not Over 'Till the Gavel Pounds—Don't date until you are officially divorced.

2.  Don't Date Until You're Ready—Don't set yourself up for more heartache because you haven't healed yet. Haven't you had enough of that heartbreak stuff already?

3.  You Catch What You Fish For—Pay attention to the pond you're fishing in, and what bait you're using.

4.  Never Ever Compromise Your Safety

5.  Get Out There!

## Chapter 20

# REMARRIAGE

"Goin' to the chapel, and we're gonna get married." Assuming that you are dating, the ultimate goal is probably marriage again at some point. But even if you're just having a good time being wined and dined with no intention of getting married, keep reading. If you haven't had a date since Jimmy Carter was in office and will never leave your house again, you can just skip this chapter.

After their divorce, some women know that they will never get married again. Sylvia spent the majority of her adult life with her ex-husband. Post-husband, she has developed a life she loves, without him—or any other man. She's happy in her social circles, with her house, and in her lifestyle. Although she recently got a chocolate Labrador retriever, she has no interest in getting married or even dating. Sylvia is thriving in her singleness. And that's a beautiful, wonderful thing!

155

Maybe this sounds really appealing to you. After my grandmother was widowed, she wasn't interested in getting married again. "Why would I want to have to cook for a man again and pick up his socks?!" Please know that if you don't want to pick up anyone's socks other than your own ever again, that's okay! Even if your friends are always pestering you to date again, you don't have to, unless you start adopting a new guinea pig every three months and going to the grocery store in your Snuggie—then you need to listen to your friends and get out of the house more.

And there's the other pendulum swing. Samantha wanted to be married so badly that she was willing to take the next guy who showed an interest in her whether he had all his teeth or not. Okay it wasn't quite that bad, but she admits to behaving pretty desperately. Thankfully she didn't get any takers, and eventually she calmed down. Several years later, she is now dating a very nice, normal man. I have no idea if he has all his teeth or not.

I ended up dating for several years after my divorce before I met the man I eventually married. And there were times during that five year span when I didn't date at all. I wasn't in a good place, I needed a break, or I was just too busy to put in the effort. And there were also times when I wanted to be dating but didn't have any good prospects.

I remember being really lonesome at times. It was hard going from being a couple to a single. I was used to sharing my life with someone. I was used to having someone to talk to and having someone else around the house. And when it was just me, Molly, and the dog and cat, there were some very quiet nights. Sometimes it was really lonely. And while God didn't take away the lonely feeling, He was faithful.

I had to learn that God was enough for me. I had to come to the place where even though I really wanted to, it would be okay if I never remarried. That's hard. I knew that longing for a husband was a good desire, even a righteous one. After all, God created the whole marriage concept, not good for man to be alone thing, etc. But I also knew that even if I never walked down the aisle again, I needed to be content in the Lord. *Lord, I'm really lonely right now. I know you are faithful and you love me, and you are enough, but I'd sure like a real live person to share my life with.*

*My grace is sufficient for you...* that pesky verse from 1 Corinthians 12:9a

*My grace is sufficient for you, my child.* And it was. His grace was sufficient. But it would be a lie to say there still weren't lonely times.

Why do I share that? To encourage you in your loneliness, but also to warn you. If you are getting married to fill a void that belongs to God, you are not ready yet. If sheer loneliness is the driving factor for you to get married, call your friends to hang out, but don't push for a wedding. Do not expect a husband to do what only God can.

We've all heard the scary statistics about how many marriages end in divorce. Half, a little under half, a bit over half. Whatever the exact stat at this moment, it's not good. And you've probably heard that second marriages fare even worse. Why? Because people date too soon, get married before they're ready, and don't fix the issues that contributed to their divorce in the first place.

Chances are, if you're human, that even though your ex was probably much worse, you probably weren't perfect in your first marriage either. Take an honest look at some of your flaws, and then make sure you've fixed them so you're not bringing them into your next marriage. Were you a chronic, secret spender, buying splurge items behind his back? Are you still doing that in your new relationship? Mayday mayday! Did you spend too much time with your girlfriends who never really liked him in the first place? Instead of working on your marriage with your husband, did you try group therapy/bashing over cocktails? You need to deal with that. Your new husband doesn't deserve your old baggage. Fess up to destructive behavior and fix it now. Give your new marriage every opportunity to start out on a good foot. This is the primary reason the majority of second marriages fail: the issues that broke up the first marriage were never dealt with, and they reappear to wreak havoc all over again. We all know how much fun going through that first divorce was. Don't sign up for that journey again.

My second husband, Rick, and I went through a great book together called *Saving Your Second Marriage*. It helped us look at our family histories, our expectations in marriage, and our individual strengths and weaknesses. It helped us work through some potential pitfalls and also reassured us we weren't doomed to repeat the past. There are many helpful books out there designed to strengthen your marriage before it even starts. Build a strong foundation for your marriage, do the pre-marital counseling, and fill out the questionnaires. Take the time to invest in your marriage long before you start planning the wedding. Do everything you can to ensure that this time around, your marriage will endure.

You've got your emotional act together—hooray! And you've waited for not just the next guy, but the right guy. You've done the prep work and are laying a strong foundation for your marriage. Now you've got to tell the kids. How do you let your children know that it's serious and hopefully get their blessing?

When I told Molly that Rick and I were thinking

about getting married, she immediately burst into tears. That wasn't the reaction I was hoping for. My second grader liked our family how it was, and she didn't want things to change. Although she was fond of Rick, she didn't see the need for us to get married. I explained to her that, even though I loved her very much, there were times when I was lonely. I loved our little life together, but I also wanted to share it with another adult. When Molly learned to ride her bike, I was the only one cheering her on in the driveway. And I was the only one who got to enjoy her wonderment at the glitter trail left by the tooth fairy. I wanted someone to share those moments with. By God's grace, Molly understood. She wanted me to be happy too. That wasn't the last time we talked about it, but that was a turning point for her.

There is no one right answer here, no perfect conversation or script to follow. Every child is different and how your divorce affected them will be different. There are a myriad of really great books on how to do the parent/step-parenting thing and do it well. See the appendix for some suggestions. Hopefully your kids and his kids are excited about your marriage. They want to see you happy, and they like him. But if this is not quite your case, know that it takes time. There are so many factors that impact how the children will view your upcoming marriage. Keep the communication lines open. If your children are young, reassure them.

If your kids are older, reassure them. If your kids are adults, reassure them. Children, no matter their age, want to know that they will be okay, and that you will be okay.

After dating for almost three years, Rick and I got married on a beach in Zihuatanejo, Mexico. His two kids and my daughter were standing at our side. We were surrounded by our dear friends and family, and my brother did the ceremony. Oh what a joyous day! We stood on a massive boulder next to the ocean to say our vows—symbolizing placing our marriage on The Rock. And at the end, everyone placed their hands on us and prayed a prayer of blessing over our marriage. How good is our God? Oh Father, I praise you that you are indeed the healer of broken hearts—both for me and for the dear women reading these words.

Marriage may or may not be part of God's plan for you. Even if you're not planning on it, God has a way of surprising us sometimes. Make sure you're in the place He wants you to be if He's giving you a second chance at this. Ask yourself the hard questions, do the prep work, invest in your marriage long before the wedding. If the two of you seek God's face above all else, you will be okay. Take a deep breath, pray for God's wisdom and His protection over your marriage, and go buy yourself a bridal magazine. Congratulations!

## Chapter 21

# BLOOMS IN THE DESERT

O h sweet sister, what a journey you are on. For it is
indeed just that: a journey. And it will be an ever-
changing, up and down, surprising, exciting, painful,
joyful journey for the rest of your life. I promise it gets
easier every day. It really does. Some days, the healing
comes in the tiniest of victories like lipstick and clean
underwear, and other days the scope of healing will
take your breath away. Know that this is a process that
takes time. Bad news for you impatient sorts, but oh
so very good for the gradual healing of your wounded
spirit. Little by little, the dry parts of your soul will be
refreshed. The scorched areas where love and hope went
dormant will return to life. Ever so slowly, the waters
from heaven will seep into your desert. And one day,
where yesterday there was dry rock and burnt earth, a
blossom will burst forth.

*The desert and the parched land will be glad; the*

*wilderness will rejoice and blossom. Like the crocus, it will burst into bloom; it will rejoice greatly and shout for joy. The glory of Lebanon will be given to it, the splendor of Carmel and Sharon; they will see the glory of the LORD, the splendor of our God.* Isaiah 35:1-2 Today's New International Version

You will always have the scars of your divorce, and you will forever be changed. But how you are changed is up to you. This is your chance to make something new of yourself. This is your shot at starting over, at a new beginning. Our sweet Father is waiting for you. He's waiting to exchange His beauty for your ashes. Give over to Him the death of your marriage, your burnt hopes and dreams, and the charred remains of your very self. These are beautiful to our Lord. The ash pile is not your final stop on earth. Our Father is waiting to raise you up out of the ashes.

*...to comfort all who mourn, and provide for those who grieve in Zion—to bestow on them a crown of beauty instead of ashes, the oil of gladness instead of mourning, and a garment of praise instead of a spirit of despair. They will be called oaks of righteousness, a planting of the LORD for the display of his splendor.* Isaiah 61:2b-3

Your ashes don't belong to you anymore. God wants them. Let them go. Walk out of the ash pile and into His calling on your life. God has called you to be a

163

mighty oak of righteousness for the display of the Lord's splendor. Wow. Even if you feel like you're in the acorn stage, cling to the promises found in Isaiah. Take your ashes, mourning, and despair, and give them to God. He promises to take them from you and exchange them for a garment of praise, the oil of gladness, and a crown of beauty! Sign me up, God.

There will be difficult days, and even years, along the way. Satan is good at dredging up old fears, rekindling bitterness, and stirring up new strife. But you don't have to let him. Walk daily with the Lord. Breathe scripture in and out. Fall at the Lord's feet and cling to Him like no other. When you have a bad day, turn on worship music, leave your Bible open to verses that will help you to be strong, and call a friend for support. Remember who you are. You are a daughter of the King! Shout it out loud—give breath and sound to truth. God has walked every painful step of this journey with you. He's not about to abandon you now. He's got a crown of beauty that has your name on it. Go claim it with the knowledge that it was always yours to begin with. Sometimes you just need a pile of ashes to trade for it first.

One day, your divorce will be just a small part of your story, nothing more than faded scars that are only visible if you know where to look. Keep walking toward that day. Help others along the way as countless wounded will walk this road with you and after you. Know that God has a mighty plan for your life, and that He will use your divorce in ways you can't even imagine. Get ready for the next chapter in your life, sister. It's going to be a good one.

*I am still confident of this: I will see the goodness of the LORD in the land of the living. Wait for the LORD; be strong and take heart, and wait for the LORD. Psalm 27:13*

The goodness of the Lord in the land of the living! Not in heaven, not when your life is through, but now. You will see the goodness of the Lord in the land of the living, my sister! That's right now. Walk in this truth, dear friend. Breathe deeply in His mercy and love. Know that God is not finished with you; He is just beginning. Let Him turn your tragedy into triumph. Your best days are ahead of you, a woman refined into pure silver. Be strong, take heart, and wait for the Lord. He is ready to show you, His beloved daughter, His goodness in the land of the living. Leave the ashes behind, put on that crown of beauty that has your name on it, and hang on—it's your time to triumph!

# THANKS

When you survive a divorce, you don't do it alone. God gave me so many dear friends who cried with me, prayed with me, and made me get out, eat nachos and go shopping when it got really rough. Thank you, Heather, Kim, Christi, Betty, Janet, Maria, Jill, Cara, Barb, and my girlfriends who stood by me, loved on me, and were lights in a very dark time.

Thank you to the brave women who were willing to share their own stories of divorce and recovery in a selfless effort to encourage other struggling women. Cathy, Amy, Dawn, Julie, Monique, Jill, Alison, Cynthia, Kami—you are warriors!

Thank you to Eddie Jones from Lighthouse Publishing of the Carolinas for listening to my heart's cry to help and encourage women going through divorce. And sweet Amberlyn Edwards, my editor, who read, critiqued, and re-read every word I wrote and lived to tell about it. Thank you to the entire team at LPC for believing in me and so many other fantastic authors.

Thank you, Lin Johnson and the Write to Publish Writers Conference. Your passion and tireless efforts at linking writers with publishers have made this writer's dream come true.

Thank you to my long-suffering critique group—Lara, Sharla, Jan, and Jessica. Thank you for your invaluable insight, wisdom, and sharp eyes. This book came into being because of your encouragement and your faithfulness.

Thank you, Susan. I am so blessed that God caused our paths to cross when we needed each other the most. We have been through it all together. And I think we turned out pretty darn good!

Thank you to my family. Mom and Dad, you were and continue to be my example and my rock. Thank you for being a safe place of unconditional love. Joel and Michael, I love you with all my heart.

And finally, the two greatest loves of my life.

I love you, Rick. Thank you for being a man among men. Thank you for loving the Lord above all else. And thank you for being a wonderful husband and stepfather. I'm so thankful we get to see God's redeeming love together, this side of eternity.

And Molly. I love you my sweet child. You are my joy. I am so proud of you and cannot wait to see the amazing future God has for you. May He give you the desires of your heart.

# Resources & Appendix

General Information

*Nolo's Essential Guide to Divorce, 4<sup>th</sup> Edition*, June 2012, by Attorney Emily Doskow

Divorce Support & Encouragement

*Live, Laugh, Love Again* by Carla Sue Nelson, Connie Wetzell, Michelle Borquez, and Rosalind Spinks-Seay

*When He Leaves* by Kari West and Noelle Quinn

*When the Vow Breaks* by Joseph Warren Kniskern

*When I Do Becomes I Don't* by Laura Petherbridge

*Growing Through Divorce* by Jim Smoke

*Life After Divorce Revised & Updated* by Sharon Wegscheider-Cruse

*Healing Within the Storm* by Lillian Landis

Single Parenthood

*The Complete Single Mother* by Andrea Engber and Leah Flungness, Ph.D.

*Joint Custody With a Jerk* by Julie Ross and Judy Corcoran

*Mom's House, Dad's House* by Isolina Ricci Ph.D.

*Helping Children Survive Divorce* by Dr. Archibald D. Hart

Marriage Help/Re-Marriage

*Preparing for Marriage* by David Boehi, Brent Nelson, Jeff Schulte & Lloyd Shadrach

*Saving Your Second Marriage Before It Starts* by Drs. Les and Leslie Parrott

*Marriage 101* by Jewell R. Powell

*Love Must Be Tough* by Dr. James Dobson

*Tough Talk to a Stubborn Spouse* by Stephen Schwambach

*Loving Your Marriage Enough to Protect It* by Jerry B. Jenkins

*Relationship Rescue* by Phillip C. McGraw Ph.D.

*Single, Married, Separated & Life After Divorce* by Myles Munroe

*Settling for Less than God's Best?* by Elsa Kok


Spiritual Growth

*Hope for the Troubled Heart* by Billy Graham

*Fatal Distractions* by Joyce L. Rodgers

*The Shelter of God's Promises* by Sheila Walsh

*Loving God with All Your Mind* by Elizabeth George

*A Woman with a Past* by Elsa Kok

*A Woman who Hurts, A God That Heals* by Elsa Kok

*A Woman's Walk with God* by Sheila Cragg, (Devotional)

*A Woman's Pilgrimage of Faith* by Sheila Cragg, (Devotional)

Men

*Runaway Husbands* by Vikki Stark

*Men in Midlife Crisis* by Jim Conway

*What Your Husband Isn't Telling You* by David Murrow


Websites

DivorceCare – www.divorcecare.org

Stephen Ministries – www.stephenministries.org

National Domestic Abuse Hotline – 1-800-799-SAFE (7233)
www.thehotline.org

Christian Mingle – www.christianmingle.com

eHarmony – www.eharmony.com


Chapter 5

*Genesis 28:15

Joshua 1:5

Deuteronomy 31:6

Deuteronomy 31:8

John 14:18

Back Cover Statistic - U.S. Census Bureau, Statistical Abstract of the
United States: 2012

CPSIA information can be obtained at www.ICGtesting.com
Printed in the USA
LVOW05s1910271114

415840LV00036B/2139/P

9 781938 499746